People Who Died During Sex

Also by Karl Shaw

Gross
Gross 2
The Mammoth Book of Eccentrics
The Mammoth Book of Tasteless Lists
Royal Babylon

Comedy equals tragedy
plus timing.

—ANONYMOUS

Broadway
Books
New York

People Who Died
During Sex

5

&
100
Other
Terribly
Tasteless
Lists

Karl
Shaw

PUBLISHED BY BROADWAY BOOKS

Copyright © 2007 by Karl Shaw.

All Rights Reserved

Published in the United States by Broadway Books, an imprint of
The Doubleday Broadway Publishing Group, a division of
Random House, Inc., New York.

www.broadwaybooks.com

Portions of this book appeared in *The Mammoth Book of Tasteless Lists,*
The Mammoth Book of Eccentrics, Gross, and *Gross 2.*

Library of Congress Cataloging-in-Publication Data
is on file with the Library of Congress

ISBN: 978-0-7679-2059-9

PRINTED IN THE UNITED STATES OF AMERICA

1   3   5   7   9   10   8   6   4   2

FIRST EDITION

Contents

Chapter Nine: End Notes

Introduction

It all began with Queen Caroline's bowels. I found them while reading a book about King George II. His wife Caroline, it appears, could swear like a trouper, but she showed remarkable composure when she was at the receiving end of a badly bungled attempt to cure her neglected strangulated hernia in 1737. After her operation, as she lay in bed surrounded by courtiers, her bowel burst open, showering excrement all over the bed and the floor. One of her courtiers said that she hoped the relief would do her majesty some good; the Queen replied calmly that she hoped so too, because that was probably the last evacuation she would ever have. Upon her death soon afterward, the great poet Alexander Pope was moved to write:

> Here lies wrapt in forty thousand towels
> The only proof that Caroline had bowels.

Gripping stuff, but there was more. Her husband King George (grandfather of the "mad" one who lost the colonies) was an inveterate gambler and would bet on anything that moved, but he lost his appetite for it when he found out that his loyal subjects were laying bets at odds of 10–1 that he would be dead within the year. In fact, he lived on a while longer than some had hoped, eventually dying on the toilet, Elvis-style, while straining to overcome his king-sized constipation.

I was hooked. What about that poem—didn't you lose your head for that kind of thing? And what were those royal doctors doing while the Queen was redecorating her bedroom? Had there been any more hideous royal deaths? What about embarrassing deaths in general? How many famous people died during, um, sex?

Books about exploding bowels are rarely bestsellers, but I couldn't resist writing one anyway—a celebration of the grotesque aesthetic, of life's cultural underbelly; a compendium of wicked and indelicate facts. I soon discovered that in sixteenth-century Europe it was conventional for men to greet female guests by fondling their breasts—providing they were related, of course; that when Alexander the Great died his body was preserved in a large jar of honey; that some South American cannibals believed you could cure a limp by eating someone else's good leg; that Samuel Pepys chronicled his daily life in the minutest detail, but only once in nine years does he mention either himself or his wife taking a bath; and that in the Indian state of Baroda, the Maharajah had criminals executed by having elephants step on their heads. Wow.

Bad taste is a wonderful thing. Where would good taste be without it? The following is dedicated to the heroes and heroines of bad taste, including E. Mackerchar, author of *The Romance of Leprosy*; to the poet Dante Gabriel Rossetti, who had his late wife exhumed after seven years to recover an unpublished manuscript; to the inquisitive Roman emperor Frederic II, who butchered his dinner guest so that he could study the human digestive system; to George Appel, the murderer of a New York policeman and of a pun, who observed as he was being strapped into the electric chair, "Pretty soon you're going to see a baked Appel"; and to the late Lord Erskine of Rerrick, who bequeathed his testicles to the Bank of Scotland because it had "no balls."

Enjoy!

People Who Died During Sex

Chapter One

Choice Cuts

Goat's Testicles to Go:
Ten National Delicacies

1   Cena Molida (contains roasted mashed cockroaches) [Belize]

2   Fried, roasted, or boiled guinea pig [Ecuador]

3   Rat meat sausages [Philippines]

4   Desiccated petrified deer's penis [China]

5   Boodog (goat broiled inside a bag made from the carefully cut and tied goatskin: the goat is either barbecued over an open fire or cooked with a blowtorch) [Mongolia]

6   Monkey toes [Indonesia]

7   Larks' tongues [England (sixteenth century)]

8   Salted horsemeat sandwiches [Netherlands]

9   Durian fruit (has a fragrance identical to that of a rotting corpse) [Southeast Asia]

10 Khachapuri, the traditional cheese pie of the former Soviet republic of Georgia. In 1995 authorities closed down a bakery whose specialty was khachapuri when it emerged that the pies were being baked in the Tbilisi morgue.

Food for Thought:
Ten Great Gourmands

1 EMPEROR ELAGABALUS Even in an age of culinary
surprises, the emperor shocked his guests with the
novelty of the dishes on offer at his 12-hour banquets by
serving up camel brains, the combs from live chickens,
peacock and nightingale tongues, mullets' livers,
flamingos' and thrushes' brains, parrots', pheasants', and
peacocks' heads, and sows' udders. He also served his
guests exact replicas of the food he was eating, made out
of wood, ivory, pottery, or stone. The guests were
required to indulge his practical joke and continue
eating. He ate as Romans often did, reclining on couches
scattered with lilies and violets, feasting between bouts of
self-induced vomiting and demanding sex between
courses. A couple of dinner guests once complimented
him on the flower arrangement in the middle of the
imperial table and carelessly conjectured how pleasant it
might be to be smothered in the scent of roses. The
Emperor obliged: The next time they sat down to eat
with him he had them smothered to death under several
tons of petals.

2 JOHN MONTAGU, FOURTH EARL OF
SANDWICH In 1762, Britain's First Lord of the
Admiralty, a notorious gambler, gave his name to the
world's best-known convenience food when he placed a
slice of beef between two pieces of bread so that he
could carry on eating at the gaming tables without the
distraction of greasy fingers. It was not, however, for his
peerless snack that Montagu became the talk of the
taverns. When he wasn't gambling or helping lose the

4

Revolutionary War, Montagu was caricatured by the press as a notorious philanderer who was said to spend his evenings in a private "garden of lust" featuring hedges pruned to resemble a woman's private parts.

3   KING GEORGE IV The poet Leigh Hunt was sent to prison for libel when he dared to suggest that the then–Prince of Wales was overweight, but Hunt was only stating the obvious. The new king, who was fond of hosting one-hundred-course feasts, got his reign off to a flying start at his coronation banquet when he served up to his guests 7,442 pounds of beef, 7,133 pounds of veal, 2,474 pounds of mutton, and an unweighed mountain of lamb and poultry. This orgy of conspicuous consumption so offended his subjects that coronation banquets were banned forthwith. By early middle age George had a fifty-inch waist and it took three hours to squeeze him into the royal corset, and a pulley system was required to enable him to mount a horse. Even on his deathbed, his appetite was undiminished. Shortly before expiring from cardiac and respiratory problems at the age of sixty-seven, he ordered two pigeons, three steaks, a bottle of wine, a glass of champagne, two glasses of port, and a glass of brandy.

4   KING LOUIS XVIII The French Bourbon kings were all thought to have suffered from a family overeating disorder. Before he lost his appetite and his head, the ample Louis XVI, known to his courtiers as "the fat pig," was such a prolific gourmand that his gut was rumored to be infested with a giant tapeworm. Younger brother

King Louis XVIII, the largest of all the Bourbons, thought that he could deflect attention from his enormous girth by dressing in diamond-studded clothes. In the last years of his reign he suffered from a variety of illnesses, including gout, and he became completely disabled. He was in such a state of physical decay that one evening in 1823, as his valets were removing the king's shoes, a gouty toe accidentally came away with his sock.

5 WILLIAM BUCKLAND In 1824, the British vicar and geologist became the first person to identify a dinosaur fossil when he published *Notice on the Megalosaurus or Great Fossil Lizard of Stonesfield*. Buckland spent a lifetime indulging bizarre gastronomic experiences. He dined on rodents, insects, crocodile, hedgehog, mole, and roast joint of bear and puppy, and he once boasted that he was prepared to eat anything organic, although he confessed that he could not be tempted to try second helpings of stewed mole or bluebottle, a common housefly. Buckland made culinary history when he ate the embalmed heart of King Louis XIV. The organ, stolen from the king's tomb during the French Revolution, changed hands several times until it found its way into a snuffbox owned by Buckland's friend, Lord Harcourt. Buckland noted later that the heart would probably have tasted better had it been served with gravy made from the blood of a marmoset.

6 JAMES "DIAMOND JIM" BRADY The millionaire railway tycoon tried to eat his way through an estimated

$12 million fortune in the early twentieth century, mostly at fashionable New York City hotels. Starting the day with a breakfast of hominy grits, eggs, cornbread, muffins, pancakes, lamb chops, fried potatoes, beefsteak, and a gallon of orange juice, a mid-morning snack of two or three dozen oysters was followed by a lunch of clams, oysters, boiled lobsters, deviled crabs, a joint of beef, and various pies. Afternoon tea comprised a large plate of seafood washed down with several quarts of lemonade. Diamond Jim's appetite reached a peak at dinner when he consumed two or three dozen oysters, six crabs, several bowls of green turtle soup, six or seven lobsters, two ducks, a double serving of turtle meat, a sirloin steak, vegetables, and orange juice, followed by several plates of cakes and pies and a two-pound box of candy. The owner of his favorite restaurant, Charles Rector's, an exclusive establishment on Broadway, described Diamond Jim as his "best 25 customers."

7   GIOACCHINO ROSSINI The life and works of the great Italian composer were greatly influenced by food. "Di Tanti Palpiti," the most popular opera aria of its time, was familiarly known as the "rice aria" because Rossini dashed it off while waiting for his risotto to cook one day in Venice. Similarly, Rossini is said to have composed the aria "Nacqui all'Affanno e al Pianto" in *Cinderella* in less than twenty minutes in a tavern in Rome while drinking with friends. By his mid-thirties he had written thirty-nine operas and was the most acclaimed musician of his day, but then he suddenly

went into early "retirement," and spent the rest of his life throwing dinner parties at his home in Paris. Rossini claimed to have shed tears only three times in his life: the first time over his first opera, the second when he heard Paganini play the violin, and the third when his picnic lunch fell overboard on a boating trip. Rossini is now as well known for the steak named after him, created at the Café Anglais in Paris.

8   CHARLES DARWIN The great scientist displayed an early taste for natural history as a student at Cambridge University when he presided over the Glutton Club, which met weekly in order to seek out and eat "strange flesh." They dined on hawk and bittern, but after eating a particularly stringy old brown owl, they gave up and elected to get drunk on port instead. When Darwin set sail on the *Beagle* he was happy to tuck into armadillos, which "taste and look like duck," and an unnamed, twenty-pound, chocolate-colored rodent that, he said, was "the best meat I ever tasted." One Christmas, when he realized that the fowl he was eating was an extremely rare "petise," he jumped up in the middle of the meal and tried to scrape together the remaining wing, head, and neck for experiments.

9   SYLVESTER GRAHAM Inventor of the graham cracker, he believed that all health problems could be traced to sex or diet and spent a lifetime crusading against masturbation and poor eating habits. Graham was mainly concerned with the carnal passions provoked by meat-eating, theorizing that the stomach, as the major

organ of the body, was also the seat of all illness, and that hunger and sexual desire were a drain on the immune system. Graham's cure-all regime was very simple: exercise to help prevent "nocturnal emissions," a proper diet to facilitate regular bowel movements, and "sexual moderation" (once a month for married couples was enough). His *Lecture to Young Men*, written in 1834, was the first of a whole genre of medical tracts on the perils of masturbation, which were said to lead to a variety of health problems, including "a body full of disease" and "a mind in ruins." His theories influenced a generation of diet experts, including John Harvey Kellogg, inventor of the cornflake.

10 PRESIDENT WILLIAM HOWARD TAFT

A morbidly obese 320 pounds when he came to office, Taft's sole dietary concession was to give up bacon because it gave him heartburn. He owned a special bathtub big enough for four average-sized men but got stuck in it on his Inauguration Day and had to be pried out.

Cereal Killers:
Ten Food-Related Deaths

A.D. 54:   Roman emperor Claudius chokes on a feather he has been using to tickle his gullet to induce vomiting at a banquet.

1135:   King Henry I dies after eating "a surfeit of lampreys"—an eel-like fish.

1190:   Genghis Khan kills his brother in an argument over a fish.

1580:   Czar Ivan the Terrible enjoys tipping boiling-hot soup over the head of his court jester. When the jester screams in pain, Ivan runs a sword through him.

1593:   Christopher "Kit" Marlowe, the second-most gifted Elizabethan playwright after Shakespeare, is stabbed to death through the eye in a tavern during an argument over the bill.

1616:   Francis Bacon, English scientist and statesman, dies inventing frozen food. While traveling in a coach one winter's day, he suddenly realizes that food might be preserved by freezing; while stuffing a dead chicken with snow he catches a fatal chill.

1818:   Abraham Lincoln's mother, Nancy, dies after drinking milk supplied by the family dairy cow, which had recently dined on poisonous mushrooms.

1941:   Sherwood Anderson, writer, dies after accidentally swallowing a toothpick while enjoying nibbles at a cocktail party on an ocean liner bound for Brazil.

1978:   Frenchman Noël Carriou admits to killing both of his
        wives because they were poor cooks. The fifty-four-
        year-old Carriou is sentenced to eight years in jail
        after killing the second for cooking him an overdone
        roast. Seventeen years earlier he had broken his first
        wife's neck after she served him an undercooked
        meal. In passing sentence, the judge sympathizes with
        Carriou: good cooking, he agrees, is an important part
        of married life.

1994:   Peter Weiller, a German filmgoer, is beaten to death
        by ushers in a Bonn cinema because he brought his
        own popcorn.

Twelve Faddish Diets

1 Benito Mussolini lived mostly on milk, drinking up to
three quarts a day to subdue his dreadful stomachache.
When he met Hitler, however, he was careful to eat alone
so as not to reveal his strange diet because he thought it
was a bit "unfascist."

2 Henry Ford took to eating weed sandwiches every day
when he heard that the American scientist and dietitian
George Washington Carver did the same.

3 In 1644, the Danish author Theodore Reinking wrote a
book lamenting the diminished fortunes of the Danes
after their defeat by their neighbor Sweden in the Thirty
Years' War. It offended the Swedes so much that he was
imprisoned for life. After several years in jail, however,
he was given a straight choice: eat your book or lose your
head: He chose to eat his words.

4 In exile, the Ugandan dictator Idi Amin was known as
"Dr. Jaffa," an affectionate title deriving from his
excessive consumption of Jaffa oranges. A former
cannibal, Amin had become a fruitarian in his twilight
years. He had been a reluctant cannibal, though; he said
he found human flesh "too salty."

5 Hitler became a vegetarian in 1931 when his doctors put
him on a meatless diet to cure him of flatulence and a
chronic stomach disorder, but he often lapsed. According
to his cook, he was partial to sausages and stuffed pigeon.

6 The ancient sailors of Spain and Portugal regularly ate
rat meat on long voyages. The crew on board Magellan's

ship during his ill-fated attempt to circumnavigate the world sold rats to each other for one ducat each.

7   An eleventh-century order of monks, the Cathars, frowned on all forms of procreation, but they practiced frequent and savage flagellation and sodomy, neither of which they considered sinful because neither involved risk of pregnancy. The Cathars were also vegetarians on the grounds that animals were produced by sexual intercourse and that their flesh was therefore sinful. They did, however, eat plenty of fish in the mistaken belief that fish do not copulate.

8   A craze for swallowing live goldfish began at Harvard College in Cambridge, Massachusetts in 1939 when a student, Lothrop Withington, enjoyed a fishy snack to win a $10 bet. His friends told the college newspaper about it, and the Boston newspapers picked up the story. Throughout the spring of 1939, the U.S. goldfish population nosedived as students all over the country vied to outdo each other in the consumption of finny comestibles. An unofficial record for goldfish-swallowing was established—forty-three in one sitting—although the teenager who accomplished this was kicked out of his school for "conduct unbecoming to a student."

9   Ernest Hemingway wrote most of his works on a diet of peanut butter sandwiches.

10   In 1994, fisherman Renato Arganza was rescued after spending several days at sea clinging to a buoy after his

boat capsized off the Philippines. He survived by eating his underpants.

11   Sir Atholl Oakeley (1900–1987) was Britain's first professional wrestling baronet. Sir Atholl, short for a wrestler at 5' 9", was however very stout, having built up his body by religiously drinking eleven pints of milk a day for three years. This dedicated diet was adopted on the advice of his idol, a giant wrestler called Hackenschmidt, who later confessed to Sir Atholl that the quantity of milk had in fact been a misprint: The correct amount was only one pint per day.

12   Scornful of reports that his people didn't have enough to eat, the dictator Nicolae Ceauşescu complained that Romanians ate too much and introduced the revolutionary Ceauşescu Diet, a "scientific" regimen mysteriously free of the protein-rich staples Romanians missed most, especially meat and dairy products. To show that production targets were actually being met, he also staged visits to the countryside, where he was filmed inspecting displays of meat and fruit. The film crews alone knew that the food was mostly made from wood and polystyrene.

History's
Ten Least Appealing
Dinner Dates

1 MARY MALLON Also known as "Typhoid Mary,"
Mallon was the world's most notorious disease carrier. In
her capacity as a New York cook before World War I, she
was personally responsible for fifty-three separate
outbreaks of typhoid involving 1,300 people, which
resulted in at least three deaths. She regularly changed
her name to confuse health officials. She spent the last
twenty-three years of her life detained in quarantine in a
state hospital, protesting her innocence to the end.

2 ANNE BOLEYN The second wife of King Henry VIII
had a distressing habit, first observed during her
coronation banquet, of vomiting between courses. She
employed a lady-in-waiting whose job it was to hold up a
sheet and catch the royal spew whenever the Queen
looked like she was about to throw up.

3 EMPEROR SHIH HU OF CHINA (A.D. 334–349)
Banquets in the Imperial court were a trial for the
Emperor's guests but particularly bad news for the ladies
in his harem. He would select a concubine, have her
beheaded, and then serve her cooked torso to his visitors.
Keen to impress, Shih Hu also insisted on passing the
uncooked head around on a platter for his guests'
inspection so he could prove that he hadn't sacrificed his
ugliest mistress.

4 CZAR PETER THE GREAT Said to have the table
manners of a baptized bear, the Czar liked to trample
across banquet tables, treading on dishes and cutlery as
he went, with his unwashed feet. Russia's first book of

mealtime etiquette wasn't published until several years after his death. It was written by the Romanov empress Anne, who had revolutionary ideas about good manners and wanted to keep up with European standards of refined taste. Entitled *The Honest Mirror of Youth*, the slim volume advised discerning Russians how to use a knife and fork, when not to spit on the table, not to jab their elbows into their seating partners during formal dinners, and not to place their feet in guests' dishes while standing on the dining table.

5   DR. SAMUEL JOHNSON The literary giant had a voracious appetite coupled with appalling table manners and—always guaranteed to break the ice at dinner parties—Tourette's syndrome. Johnson's favorite dish was a vast pudding containing beefsteaks, kidneys, oysters, larks, and mushrooms. According to his biographer, James Boswell, he swilled, gorged, and stuffed himself until sweat ran down his cheeks and the veins stood out on his forehead. Johnson's eating habits were so disturbing that sometimes when he was invited to dine with some prominent person he would eat behind a screen.

6   MRS. BEETON Her famous *Book of Cookery and Household Management*, regarded as the housewife's culinary bible for years after it was first published in 1861, contained several potentially lethal recipes.

7   KING LOUIS XIV OF FRANCE Although the best-known portraits of Louis XIV portray him as a dapper

little man, in old age he became morbidly obese. In his later years he struggled to eat because his doctors, while removing several of his bad teeth, had accidentally broken his upper jaw and smashed his palate; from then on Louis always had difficulty chewing, and bits of food often came down his nose.

8   JUAN PERÓN By the time the Argentinean dictator's wife Eva died of cancer in 1952, an eminent pathologist had been on standby for two weeks to embalm her. With Eva barely dead, he quickly filled her veins with alcohol, then glycerin, which kept her organs intact and made her skin appear almost translucent. Juan planned to have her housed in a giant new mausoleum, but he was forced to suddenly flee the country, and the body disappeared for several years. In 1971, however, Juan and Eva were touchingly reunited, and from that day on, Eva's corpse was always present at the Perón family dinner table.

9   JEAN-BÉDEL BOKASSA The cannibal former president of the Central African Republic once served political opponents up to unwitting visiting dignitaries as "roast beef."

10   IDI AND SARAH AMIN In 1999, London restaurateur Sarah Amin, the ex-wife of former Ugandan dictator Idi, was found to be running a kitchen with a "heavy and active" cockroach and mouse infestation, and her establishment was closed down by health officials. She was, at least, a better fellow dining prospect than her husband. Guests at the home of Uganda's president were

treated to some unscheduled entertainment by their host
one evening in August 1972, when between courses Amin
suddenly vanished into the kitchen and returned with
the frozen head of his former commander in chief,
Brigadier Hussein. Amin screamed abuse and threw
silverware at the head, then asked his guests to leave.

T𝑒𝑛 Historic Drunks

1   NOAH According to the Old Testament, Noah was the first person ever to get drunk.

2   KING SCORPION I OF EGYPT The Pharaohs loved their wine. In 3500 B.C., his royal highness's cadaver was entombed with seven hundred bottles of resin-infused hooch to help ease his journey into the afterlife.

3   SOCRATES (469–399 BC) The great philosopher had a legendary ability to hold his liquor and would continue to philosophize when everyone else at the symposium had long since passed out or gone home.

4   ALEXANDER THE GREAT (356–323 BC) The Macedonian king who ruled an empire stretching from Greece to India was in his lifetime as famous for his marathon drinking sessions as for his military conquests. During one of Alexander's drinking contests thirty-five men died; during another he killed one of his best friends with a spear. His close friend Hephaestion expired after drinking half a gallon of wine for breakfast; Alexander dropped dead after a drinking contest at the age of thirty-two.

5   POPE BENEDICT XII (C. 1334–42) The pontiff was such a hardened boozer that the expression "drunk as a pope" became popular in his lifetime.

6   SELIM II, SULTAN OF THE OTTOMANS (R. 1566–74) Also known as "Selim the Sot," he could drink a bottle of Cyprus wine without drawing a breath. When he ran out of his favorite drink, someone

suggested he capture Cyprus to replenish his stocks. Selim agreed and massacred thirty thousand Cypriot Christians in the process.

7 **EMPRESS CATHERINE I, CZARINA OF RUSSIA (R. 1725–27)** While shuffling through her two-year reign in a drunken haze, she once survived an assassination attempt, too drunk to realize that anything had happened. She was reviewing a Guards regiment when a bullet flew past her and struck an innocent bystander dead. The Empress moved on without flinching.

8 **LUDWIG VAN BEETHOVEN (1770–1827)** The composer died of hepatic cirrhosis of the liver as a result of alcoholism at the age of fifty-seven. Before he expired, he cheerily announced, "Wine is both necessary and good for me."

9 **PRESIDENT ANDREW JOHNSON, U.S. PRESIDENT (1865–69)** He was apparently drunk at his swearing-in as vice president to Lincoln, and his acceptance speech was rambling and largely incoherent; he claimed later that he had been taking alcoholic medicine prescribed for a cold. He didn't make his own inaugural address: When the U.S. chief justice was sent to tell him that Lincoln was dead and that he was now president, they found him trying to shake off a terrible hangover. Johnson took the oath of office as required but then fell asleep and had to be dressed and carried to the White House.

10 SIR WINSTON CHURCHILL (1874–1965) Britain's
great wartime leader began each day with a glass of
Riesling with his breakfast, then kept himself topped up
with whiskey until the early hours of the following day.
A doctor attending him after he was knocked down by a
car in New York in 1931 actually issued a medical note
that his convalescence "necessitates the use of alcoholic
spirits especially at mealtimes," specifying 250cc per day
as the minimum. Although it wrecked his health, he
liked to brag, "I have taken more out of alcohol than
alcohol has taken out of me."

T*e*n Exclusive Beverages

1.   Three Penis Wine, one of several multi-penis wines produced in China, is made from one part seal penis, one part dog penis, and four parts deer penis. Said to be an elixir of great repute for flagging lovers, it is also an allegedly effective cure for anemia, shingles, and memory loss.

2.   The world's most exclusive beverage is made from a coffee bean that has passed through the digestive tract of a cat. The excretions of the palm civet cat are collected from around the coffee plantations of Indonesia and are sold at around $75 a cup. Luckily for coffee drinkers, the palm civet ingests only the very ripest beans, and then internal fermentation by enzymes adds a unique flavor and removes a source of coffee's natural bitterness. The beans are then passed whole and unsullied into the cat's poo.

3.   The Yukon Territory in Canada is the home of the Sour Toe Cocktail, which has only two ingredients: an amputated human toe and the spirit of your choice. The only rule is "you can drink it fast, you can drink it slow, but the lips have got to touch the toe." The original artifact, discovered in a disused log cabin by a Mountie in 1973, was used in the drink more than seven hundred times before it was accidentally swallowed by a miner.

4.   The Tomb of Mausalus, one of the Seven Wonders of the World, destroyed by earthquake, was built in 353 B.C. in Turkey by Queen Artemisia on the death of her husband, King Mausalus. The king's body was to have been placed

in the tomb but there was a last minute change of plan. His wife had him cremated, then she poured his ashes into a goblet of wine and drank the lot. (We memorialize Mausalus today with our word "mausoleum.")

5   Cow urine is sold in India as a sedative; as a cure for cancer, AIDS, tuberculosis; and as an antiseptic aftershave.

6   In 1885, the U.S. army captain and part-time naturalist John Bourke published a detailed description of the Urine Dance of the Zuni Indians of New Mexico. Bourke related how he had been privileged to witness this unique ritual, which involved a dozen Zuni Indians dancing around a fire while drinking several gallons of fresh urine. When the Zuni invited their guests to participate in a similar ceremony, this time involving human excrement, Bourke made his excuses and left.

7   After the Great Fire of London in 1666, the remains of the former Dean of St. Paul's, John Colet, were rescued from the cathedral where they had lain since 1509. Although protected by a lead-lined coffin, it was noted by two gentlemen called Wyld and Greatorex that the Dean's remains had become cooked in his preserving fluids and had dissolved into a soupy substance. They sampled the "soup" and declared that it tasted "only of iron."

8   When Britain's great naval hero Admiral Horatio Nelson died, his corpse was placed in a keg of brandy to preserve

it on the long journey home. Although Nelson's body bubbled away in it for days, that didn't prevent his crew from drinking the spirits later.

9   The Cocoma tribe of Peru drank the ground-up bones of a deceased relative in a fermented brew. They believed that it was much better for the dead to be inside a warm friend than outside in the cold earth.

10   Adolf Hitler once attempted to cure his chronic flatulence by drinking machine-gun oil.

Ten 10 Alternative
Uses for Coca-Cola

1   As a spermicide [India]

2   As a pesticide [India]

3   As a toilet bowl cleaner

4   As a windshield washer

5   As a rust-spot remover

6   As a bloodstain remover

7   As a grease-stain remover

8   As a sink cleaner

9   As a meat tenderizer

10   As a wallpaper-paste remover

Waiting for a Grill Like You:
Ten Human Recipes

1   Adolph Luetgert, a Chicago master butcher in the 1870s, was fired by a driving ambition to make his sausages famous all over America. Luetgert's dream came true when he was arrested and tried for the murder of his wife Louisa after disposing of her corpse by melting it down in one of his giant vats and incorporating her into his sausage production line. For two years after Luetgert's conviction, sausage sales in Illinois and neighboring Michigan hit an all-time low.

2   The British explorer Captain James Cook often wrote in his journals about the cannibalistic habits of some of the natives he encountered on his trips to the South Seas. Ironically, he ended his days as a Hawaiian buffet. All that Cook's men could find of him after he had been killed and dismembered at a traditional *heianu* ceremony at Keala Kekua were a few bones and some salted flesh.

3   In 1991, Wang Guang, owner of the White Temple restaurant in China, built up a huge following for his heavily spiced Sichuan-style dumplings. Over a four-year period the exotic fillings were supplied by Guang's brother, who worked as an assistant in the local crematorium. The secret ingredient of White Temple's menu—human flesh—was exposed after police were tipped off by the parents of a young girl who had died in a road accident. When they came to cremate her body they discovered that parts of it were missing.

4   The Carib Indians of the West Indies, encountered by Columbus, were the world connoisseurs of human haute

cuisine. Caribs bred children expressly for edible purposes: the male children were castrated because it improved the flavor. According to Caribs, the best bits on a human being are the palms of the hands, the fingers, and the toes. Columbus noted that the Caribs considered the French to be the very tastiest people.

5   Marco Polo noted in 1275 that the people of Southeast Asia ate the feet of their captives, believing them to be "the most savory food in the world."

6   When the Chinese famine of 206 B.C. killed half the population, human flesh became the staple diet. The taste for people, however, lingered on long after famine conditions had gone. During the T'ang dynasty in the late ninth and tenth centuries, cannibalism was permitted by law and human flesh was sold publicly in street markets.

7   The Tartar hordes that swept across Europe in 1242 were particularly fond of girls. Appetizing young maidens were issued as rations to army officers, while common soldiers chewed on the tough flesh of older women. Breast meat was regarded as the finest tidbit and was reserved for the prince's table.

8   Fijian cannibals acquired a taste for hanks of salted human flesh—a variation on European or American chewing tobacco.

9   During World War II, the British Minister of Food, Lord Woolton, carefully considered but finally rejected a plan,

proposed by his government scientists, to feed the country on black pudding made from surplus blood-bank donations.

10   In 1977, the U.S. government staged the official grand opening ceremony of their brand-new Department of Agriculture staff canteen, which was attended by Robert Bergland, the agriculture secretary. Mr. Bergland unveiled a brass plaque naming the canteen the Alfred Packer Memorial Dining Facility after one of America's most famous nineteenth-century frontiersmen. A few months later, the plaque was removed when someone remembered what the late Mr. Packer had been chiefly famous for—killing and eating five Colorado gold prospectors in the 1870s.

Gluttons for Punishment: Twenty World Eating Records

1   50 hot dogs in 12 minutes

2   57 cow brains (18 pounds) in 10 minutes

3   3.5 pounds of cooked dog in 18 minutes, 10 seconds

4   100 yards of spaghetti in 28 seconds

5   12 slugs in 2 minutes

6   28 cockroaches in 4 minutes

7   60 earthworms in 3 minutes, 6 seconds

8   100 live maggots in 5 minutes, 29 seconds

9   2 pounds of eels in 32 seconds

10 144 snails in 11 minutes, 30 seconds

11 12 bananas (including skins) in 4 minutes, 14 seconds

12 13 raw eggs in 1.4 seconds

13 65 hard-boiled eggs in 6 minutes, 40 seconds

14 7 quarter-pound sticks of salted butter in 5 minutes

15 5.75 pounds of asparagus spears in 10 minutes

16 6 pounds 9 ounces of cabbage in 9 minutes

17 1 gallon 9 ounces of vanilla ice cream in 12 minutes

18 6 pounds of tinned Spam in 12 minutes

19 3 onions in 1 minute

20 4 32-ounce bowls of mayonnaise in 8 minutes

Chapter
Two

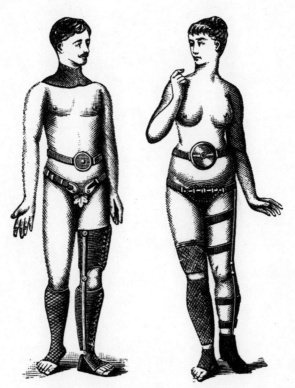

Love Hurts

Twelve Celebrity Celibates

1   KING EDWARD "THE CONFESSOR" Edward had no sexual relations at all with his wife Edith, a curious state of affairs known in theological terms as a "chaste marriage" by which Edith came to be known as a "virgin queen." There was some confusion whether Edward abstained for religious reasons or from his aversion to his wife, but tradition has it that it was the former, and Edward was duly made a saint in 1161. Some of Edith's contemporaries were less sure of her virginity.

2   SIR ISAAC NEWTON A lifelong bachelor and rigidly puritanical, he was said to have laughed just once in his life, when someone asked him what use he saw in Euclid. He severed all relations with a friend who once told him an off-color joke about a nun.

3   NIKOLA TESLA The Serbian-American scientist who invented AC power transmission avoided all romantic entanglements, believing that sex was a drain on creativity. When asked by a reporter why he never married, Tesla replied, "I do not think you can name many great inventions that have been made by married men."

4   HANS CHRISTIAN ANDERSEN The fairy-tale writer made highly publicized declarations of love for prominent, unattainable women, including the "Swedish nightingale," Jenny Lind. He also visited prostitutes, but he paid them just to sit and chat with him. He died unmarried and a virgin, so terrified of being buried alive

that he left a written request that one of his main arteries be severed before he was placed in his coffin.

5   J. M. BARRIE The creator of Peter Pan, the little boy who refused to grow up, was barely five feet tall and always blamed his short stature for his lack of success with women. In 1894, however, while seriously ill, Barrie made a dramatic deathbed marriage proposal to Mary Ansell, a beautiful actress who had starred in one of his plays. She accepted, but on their honeymoon it became apparent that the recuperating Barrie had little interest in normal marital relations. The union was never consummated.

6   LEWIS CARROLL A mathematics teacher, amateur photographer, and author of some of the great classics of children's literature, including *Alice's Adventures in Wonderland*, Carroll, whose real name was Charles Dodgson, had no relationships at all with women, although at one point there was talk of an affair with the leading actress of the day, Ellen Terry. She was dismissive of the story; when asked to comment about her reported liaison with the author, she replied, "He was as fond of me as he could be of anyone over the age of ten."

7   EDGAR DEGAS The French Impressionist painter and sculptor spent long hours gazing at naked women getting in and out of bathtubs, but he was probably impotent. One day a wealthy hostess asked him; "Why do you paint women so ugly, Monsieur Degas?" He replied, "Because, madam, women in general are ugly."

8   GEORGE FREDERIC HANDEL The unmarried German-born English musician gave away few clues about his private life. His royal patron, King George II, was one of many contemporaries who was kept guessing; when the king asked Handel why there was no Mrs. Handel, the great composer replied, "I have no time for anything but music." Handel did, however, have a stormy relationship with a close friend, the young German composer and singer Johann Mattheson. One day at the opera, he and Mattheson had a spat over who should play the harpsichord. Handel refused to budge, and a fistfight broke out in the orchestra pit.

9   SØREN KIERKEGAARD The solemn Danish philosopher considered sexual relations an abomination; "My depression," he said in one of his lighter moments, "is the most faithful mistress I have known." When he was twenty-four, however, he fell in love with a fourteen-year-old schoolgirl named Regine Olsen, and they were briefly engaged before he broke it off. Kierkegaard never really got over Regine, and over the years he tried to woo her back by bombarding her with his books of gloomy reflections. Although she never wrote back, he named her his sole beneficiary.

10   EDWARD LEAR The Victorian polymath and "nonsense poet" lived alone with his cat, writing limericks about men who he drew with long, unmistakably phallic noses. Lear's illustration for his limerick "The Old Man with a Nose," for example, shows a man poking his very long nose at three

frightened children—possibly a reference to some sexually abusive childhood experience of his own. Throughout his adult life he suffered from what he called "the Demon" or "the Morbids"—epilepsy, a state of mind that he personally attributed to excessive masturbation.

11   HENRY MORTON STANLEY The journalist and explorer became a household name when the *New York Herald* commissioned him to "find Livingstone" in Africa, which he did, with the famous greeting, "Dr. Livingstone, I presume." Stanley emerged from the nether regions of darkest Africa to marry, at the age of forty-nine, the high-society portrait painter Dorothy Tennant in a lavish wedding ceremony at Westminster Abbey, but on his wedding night he informed his wife that he considered sex "fit only for beasts." The marriage was never consummated.

12   MOHANDAS "MAHATMA" GANDHI In his thirties and long since married with children, Gandhi surprised Mrs. Gandhi by taking a vow of celibacy, explaining that total control over his "vital fluids" would enhance his spiritual powers and give him strength during his long fasts. His wife was even more surprised when in his seventies he employed a string of young women to massage him and sleep nude with him to "test" his celibacy. Not everyone understood, and he abandoned his nocturnal "experiments" when several of his followers resigned in disgust.

Tem Aphrodisiacs

A.D. 900: Sheep's eyelid marinated in hot tea. Chinese emperors were required to keep twenty-one wives, a precise number thought to have magical properties, and the emperor was expected to make love to ten of them every night. A Taoist manual advised that this could be made possible by applying the mixture to the imperial penis.

1400: Pigeon dung and snail excrement [England]

1690: Toad excrement [France]. This method had the royal seal of approval; it was the one successfully employed by King Louis XIV's mistress Madame de Montespan.

1700: Menstrual blood as a food or drink additive [Germany]

1830: Lion testicles or arsenic [London]

1850: Penis and scrotum of a vanquished enemy warrior [Brazilian Cubeo tribe]

1900: Live monkey brains [Malaysia]. The live monkey was forced into a tight container with a bowl fitted to its head, the skull was cut open and peeled back to reveal the exposed brain, which was then scooped out with a spoon or sucked through a straw.

1943: Animal hormone. To restore Adolf Hitler's impaired virility, his personal physician, Dr. Theodore Morell, injected the Führer with a compound containing hormones from crushed animal genitalia.

1950:   Chili and other hot spices. These are banned as
         prison food in some South and Central American
         countries, as they are feared likely to arouse
         passions "unseemly in a single-sex environment."

2005:   Dolphins' testicles [Japan]. Chicken testicles are
         preferred in Taiwan.

Great Balls of Fire:
F*orty* Syphilitics*

Pope Alexander VI

Thomas Aquinas

Johann Sebastian Bach

Charles Baudelaire

Al Capone

Randolph Churchill

Emperor Commodus

Captain James Cook

Hernán Cortez

Frederick Delius

Albrecht Dürer

Desiderius Erasmus

King Francis I of France

King Frederick "the Great"
of Prussia

Paul Gauguin

King George I
of Great Britain

Johann Wolfgang von Goethe

Francisco Goya

Heinrich Heine

King Henry VIII
of England

King Herod of Judea

Adolf Hitler

Czar Ivan "the Terrible"

Julius Caesar

John Keats

Pope Leo X

Ferdinand Magellan

Guy de Maupassant

John Milton

Edouard Monet

Benito Mussolini

Friedrich Nietzsche

Czar Paul I

Arthur Schopenhauer

Franz Schubert   Henri Toulouse-Lautrec

Jonathan Swift   Voltaire

Emperor Tiberius   Oscar Wilde

....

*
Syphilis was long thought to have originated in the Americas and to have begun its spread around the world after Columbus's voyage in 1492. The disease may have been in Europe before Columbus, but it became commonplace after the arrival of new strains from the New World. The first European epidemic broke out in 1494, spread in part by retreating French troops after the siege of Naples. Whatever its origins, the disease swept through the European population in the sixteenth century. At its peak in the nineteenth century, syphilis affected as much as 15 percent of the adult population of Europe and North America, but it has largely died out since the development of penicillin in the 1940s. While it is impossible to retrospectively diagnose with complete accuracy, there is evidence that syphilis afflicted everyone on this list.

This Old Heart of Mine:
Ten Horny Senior Citizens

1   KING LOUIS XIV OF FRANCE The tiny "Sun King" was renowned for his phenomenal sexual appetite: His second wife and former mistress Madame de Montespan complained to her priest that she found the effort of making love to her seventy-year-old husband twice a day very tiring.

2   VICTOR HUGO The French author of *The Three Musketeers*, *The Hunchback of Notre Dame*, and *Les Miserables* required only four hours of sleep per night— bad news for his wife, who was required to accommodate him nine times on her wedding night alone. He had a twenty-two-year-old girlfriend when he was seventy and was still sexually active when he died at eighty-three. His family tried to keep the frisky old poet from escaping into the streets in search of prostitutes, but they were not entirely successful: His diary records that he had sex four times in the final four months of his life.

3   EMPRESS CATHERINE "THE GREAT" OF RUSSIA She was both insomniac and nymphomaniac, which meant trouble for the dozens of handsome young soldiers she continued to bed well into her late sixties. She had twenty-one "official" lovers, of whom the last, Platon Zubov, was twenty-two years old when they met: She was sixty-four. Catherine's astonishing sex life, coupled with her ability to ride a horse like a man— considered shocking at a time when all women rode side-saddle—gave rise to the myth that she had sex with a horse. Catherine's frolics were eventually terminated

when she had a massive stroke and fell off her toilet seat in her sixty-seventh year.

4   THOMAS HARDY The English poet and novelist, author of *Far from the Madding Crowd*, *Tess of the D'Urbervilles*, and *Jude the Obscure*, married his thirty-five-year-old secretary Florence Dugdale when he was seventy-three. Hardy boasted to a friend that he was still capable of "full sexual intercourse" at the age of eighty-four.

5   W. B. YEATS Success came to the poet late in his life, and he suddenly found himself surrounded by adoring young women, but he was also plagued with impotence and writer's block. In an effort to revive both his flagging creative inspiration and his sex drive, he experimented with a number of quack impotence cures including a vasectomy procedure known as "Steinaching"— performed by the Viennese doctor Eugene Steinach: Six months later, Yeats got lucky with a beautiful young actress, Margot Ruddock, twenty-seven to his sixty-nine. The Dublin newspapers dubbed Yeats "the gland old man of poetry."

6   KING LUDWIG I OF BAVARIA The grandfather of "Mad" King Ludwig II achieved international notoriety at the age of sixty-one by stepping out with a notorious courtesan, twenty-eight-year-old Lola Montez: She introduced herself to the elderly monarch by ripping open her bodice and revealing her breasts. Ludwig pledged his undying love to Lola in reams of

outstandingly bad verse, but he was eventually forced by pressure from a popular uprising and his ministers to banish her from the country. Some suggested that she went willingly to escape another burst of the king's poetry.

7   LORD PALMERSTON In spite of his ill-fitting false teeth, Britain's prime minister was irresistible to women during the Crimean War. "Old Pam" or "Lord Cupid," as he was known in Parliament, fathered seven illegitimate children and once tried to rape one of Queen Victoria's ladies-in-waiting while he was visiting Windsor Castle (he later claimed he was drunk and had entered the wrong bedroom). In 1862, aged seventy-nine, he was cited as the correspondent in a divorce case. The story considerably enhanced his popularity; it was rumored that Palmerston even encouraged the gossip because he was hoping to call a general election.

8   H. G. WELLS The author of *The Time Machine*, *The Invisible Man*, and *The War of the Worlds*, Wells was an unlikely lothario, being a short, fat, balding diabetic with an overly large head and a high-pitched squeaky voice, but according to one lover his body "smelled of honey," which may have helped him have affairs into his seventies with women up to forty years younger than himself. He was still at it until his death, a month before his eightieth birthday.

9   MAO ZEDONG The Communist leader believed that he could achieve longevity by increasing the number of

his sexual partners, and well into his seventies he was still shedding his drab military uniform to bed several young women at a time. Temporary bouts of impotence were treated with injections of ground deer antlers and a secret formula called H3.

10   BERTRAND RUSSELL A Nobel prize winner and one of the greatest philosophers of the twentieth century, he had a string of high-profile affairs with married women in his seventies and enjoyed his fourth honeymoon at the age of eighty—and all this despite a childhood accident that damaged his penis when he fell out of a moving carriage. On a lecture tour of America, the elderly philosopher was asked by the dean of a respectable girls' college, "Why did you give up philosophy?" Russell replied: "Because I discovered fucking."

Ten Milestones
in Contraception

1300 B.C.: Egyptian women use pessaries made from crocodile dung.

900 B.C.: Chinese birth-control experts advise women to swallow sixteen tadpoles fried in quicksilver immediately after intercourse.

200 B.C.: Arabians eat mashed pomegranate mixed with rock salt and alum.

1100: The Dominican Church advises women to spit three times into the mouth of a frog, or to eat bees, immediately after intercourse.

1400: Italians attempt to avoid pregnancy by drinking raw onion juice.

1600: The French swear by cabbage, taken orally after intercourse.

1650: German women smear their private parts with tobacco juice.

1700: Islamic women are advised to jump backward seven or nine times immediately after sex.

1750: Europeans wear condoms made from animal offal. The original condoms are made from sausage skins by slaughterhouse workers. Casanova, who hates using condoms, places his faith in three gold balls, purchased from a Genoese goldsmith for about $90, which he places inside his partner. He claims that this method has served him well for fifteen years. A more likely explanation for his run of luck is that he is infertile.

1843:   Mr. Goodyear vulcanizes rubber. The Japanese, however, continue to wear sheaths made from leather or tortoiseshell.

T*en* Presidential Peccadilloes

1   GEORGE WASHINGTON (1789–97) The original
     "philanderer-in-chief." Among the women with whom
     Washington was known or suspected to have had
     adulterous relationships were Kitty Greene, Lucy Flucker
     Knox, Elizabeth Gates, Theodosia Prevost Burr, Kitty
     Duer, Phoebe Fraunces, Eliza Powell, Mrs. William
     Bingham, and Mrs. Perez Morton. Officially, Washington
     died of a chill that he caught, according to the official
     version, riding his horse in the snow. According to a more
     likely interpretation, he caught his death when he
     jumped out of a window trouserless after an assignation
     with an employee's wife at Mount Vernon.

2   THOMAS JEFFERSON (1801–9) He lectured his
     fellow men on the dangers of associating with women
     and "the depravation of morals and ambiguity of issue,"
     but the effect was slightly undermined by the fact that
     he slept with slave girls. Jefferson had a twenty-year
     sexual relationship with a slave called Sally Hemmings
     who was thirty years his junior. She bore him six
     children who were also kept as slaves. Jefferson also had
     adulterous affairs with Elizabeth Walker while her
     husband, General John Walker, was away fighting in one
     of the Indian Wars, and with Maria Cosway, wife of the
     famous English painter of miniatures Richard Cosway.

3   JAMES GARFIELD (1881) President Garfield said his
     marriage to his wife Lucretia was "a great mistake" and
     vowed to spend as much of his time far away from her on
     business trips as he possibly could. In 1862, he was
     caught in an affair with an eighteen-year-old reporter

47

from the *New York Times*, Lucia Calhoun. Mrs. Garfield made him choose between staying married and faithful or getting a divorce and damaging his career. Garfield chose the former, but during the 1880 election the press reported his frequent visits to a New Orleans brothel.

4   GROVER CLEVELAND (1885–89, 1893–97) Cleveland was one of the very few presidents to enter the White House a bachelor. In 1884, just as his first presidential campaign was getting under way, he was exposed as the father of an illegitimate son by a thirty-three-year-old widow, Mrs. Maria Crofts Halpin. His campaign team urged him to "lie like a gentleman," but Cleveland ignored their advice and owned up. His supporters, taunted throughout the campaign by the Republican chant "Ma, Ma, Where's My Pa," responded with "Gone to the White House, ha ha ha!" In the 1893 election, Cleveland's political enemies circulated a leaflet accusing him of bestiality, wife-beating, and "habitual immoralities with women." He was reelected with a healthy majority.

5   WARREN G. HARDING (1921–23) Ruggedly handsome and immensely popular, Harding won the presidency by the biggest popular vote margin ever, then spent his time in office conducting random adulterous affairs, including a fifteen-year relationship with Mrs. Carrie Phillips, the wife of a friend. He began an affair with a seventeen-year-old, Nan Britton, when he was fifty-three, passing her off in public as his niece. When she gave birth to his daughter, Harding tried to buy her

silence by paying her $20,000 plus a monthly allowance. It didn't stop her from cashing in with a best-selling kiss-and-tell book, published in 1927, that detailed clandestine trysts in seedy hotels, in the Senate Office building, and once, memorably, in an Oval Office cupboard. Harding died suddenly at fifty-seven on a speaking tour of Alaska; his last words were, "How do the bull seals control their extensive harems?" The news of the seemingly robustly healthy Harding's death was a shock, and a rumor attributed his death to a sexually transmitted disease. It was also claimed that he had been poisoned by his wife, Florence, possibly in revenge for twenty years of dedicated infidelity. The poisoning theory could be neither proven nor refuted, as Mrs. Harding pointedly refused to permit a postmortem examination. It may have shed some light on another, unconnected medical mystery; a White House doctor during the Harding administration once told a reporter that the president had three testicles.

6   FRANKLIN D. ROOSEVELT (1933–45) Roosevelt lost the use of his legs after being paralyzed by polio in 1921. He lost the use of his wife's legs three years earlier when she found a pile of love letters linking him to her twenty-two-year-old secretary, Lucy Page Mercer. Roosevelt promised to break off the relationship but, with his marriage effectively over, lived more or less openly with his personal secretary Marguerite "Missy" LeHand at his retreats in Florida and Warm Springs, Georgia. In 1945 the world was informed that the sixty-

three-year-old president had died of a brain hemorrhage while having his portrait painted by the artist Elizabeth Shoumatoff, a friend of Lucy Page Mercer, with whom Roosevelt had renewed his affair and was spending the weekend. According to unconfirmed reports, he actually died of a heart attack during oral sex.

7 DWIGHT D. EISENHOWER (1953–61) "Ike" had an affair with twenty-four-year-old Kay Summersby, who was assigned to be his driver during World War II and later became his personal secretary. Eisenhower told his young mistress he would divorce his wife and marry her as soon as the war was over, but he never followed through on his promise, and after the war the two lovers never saw each other again.

8 JOHN F. KENNEDY (1961–63) Kennedy is famously quoted as saying, "Ich bin ein Berliner"; less famously, "I'm never through with a girl until I've had her three ways." "Shafty" as he was known in his Navy days, enlisted White House staff to help organize the unending procession of women who participated in "entertainments" including regular nude swimming parties in the presidential pool. Kennedy attributed his confident and relaxed famous first live televised debate with Richard Nixon to the fact that he had prepared by taking horizontal refreshment with a prostitute in a nearby hotel room minutes before the cameras began to roll: JFK was so pleased with the result that he decided to repeat the trick before all his TV debates. His technique was not, however, the stuff of legend, and he was by

repute a quick and selfish lover, his efforts undermined by stress and recurring ill health; actress Angie Dickinson said her fling with the president "was the best twenty seconds of my life."

9   LYNDON B. JOHNSON (1963–69) The thirty-sixth U.S. president, by reputation a distant second in the White House adultery stakes behind the man he replaced, was said to have "the instincts of a Turkish Sultan." LBJ was genuinely aggrieved that John F. Kennedy's reputation as a stud was greater than his and complained to friends, "I've had more women by accident than he's had on purpose." The Philippine president Ferdinand Marcos was once informed by his wife, Imelda, that she was being groped by LBJ on the White House dance floor. Marcos replied, "Ignore it, Meldy. It's in a good cause."

10   WILLIAM J. CLINTON (1993–2001) In 1992, a cabaret singer from Little Rock, Arkansas, Gennifer Flowers, became the first of many former lovers to kiss and tell when she revealed intimate details about her twelve-year affair with Clinton in *Penthouse* magazine. Subsequent allegations of sexual misconduct included affairs with the wife of a judge; a salesclerk from a Little Rock department store cosmetics counter; a prostitute, Bobbie Ann Williams, who claimed that Clinton fathered her child; and a former Miss Arkansas who alleged that her affair with Clinton had ended with the offer of a $40,000-per-year job if she kept quiet and the offer of broken legs if she didn't. In 1994, Clinton's private parts

went public when a typist from Arkansas claimed that
the president had dropped his trousers and exposed
himself to her at a Democratic Party conference.
According to Paula Jones, the First Phallus had a
"distinguishing characteristic." In 1998, Clinton became
the second U.S. president to be impeached, accused of
instructing a twenty-four-year-old White House intern
named Monica Lewinsky to lie under oath. He was tried
in the Senate and found not guilty of the charges
brought against him. He apologized to the nation and
continued to have unprecedented popular approval
ratings.

The Stuff of Fairy Tales: Ten Royal Marriages

1547: Russian Czar Ivan "the Terrible" marries his first wife, Anastasia, winner of the first "Miss Russia" contest. The Czar's bride has been selected from his country's most beautiful maidens, who were summoned to the Kremlin and subjected to *smotrinya*—an intimate examination that was a cross between a beauty pageant and a customs body search. Ivan was consistently unlucky in love. The first three of his eight wives died young, the second just two weeks after the wedding day; the death of his third wife, Martha, according to one account, was brought on by Ivan's excessively enthusiastic foreplay. His fourth wife, Anna, was married to him by proxy, but "almost died of fright" at the prospect of meeting him and had to be sent to a convent. When he found out that his seventh wife, Maria, had lied to him about her virginity when he married her, he had her drowned the following day. His eighth and final wife, also named Maria, survived him: He died playing chess.

1708: King Frederick I of Prussia marries his mad third wife, Sophia. The House of Hohenzollern, the royal family of Prussia and later of Germany, believes in a family ghost; according to legend, a "white lady" will appear before the head of the household when it is time for him to die. One evening, the king's young wife charges headfirst through the glass door to his bedroom and appears before him in her white nightgown splattered in blood. Frederick took her for the family ghost, had a heart attack, and died a few days later.

1733: King Frederick II "the Great" of Prussia marries Princess Elizabeth Christine of Brünswick-Bayern. The wedding has been arranged by his psychopathic father, King Frederick William I, who suspects that his son is gay. Young Frederick, horrified by the prospect of marriage, threatens to commit suicide, but his father sends him a terse note to the effect that suicide will not be necessary, because if he doesn't do as he is told he will be executed anyway. The couple go their separate ways immediately after the wedding night.

1745: Czar Peter III of Russia marries the German princess Catherine (later Empress Catherine "the Great"). Peter finds his collection of warfare toys a much bigger attraction than his new bride and plays with his wooden soldiers, miniature cannons, and toy fortresses under the bedclothes, taking up the whole bed with war games while his virgin wife lies undisturbed beside him: Catherine draws the line when he starts to rear hunting dogs in his bedroom and she finds herself sharing their bed with ten spaniels. History records that she opts for strangulation instead of marriage guidance: Catherine led a palace revolution in which her husband was deposed and then murdered.

1765: Emperor Joseph II of Austria marries his second wife, Josepha. The Empress suffers from a skin complaint that makes her so physically repulsive to the Emperor that he has the balcony connecting his room to hers sealed off. "If I could put the tip of my finger on the tiniest point of her body that is not covered with boils," he noted, "I

54

would try to have children." There are no children,
nor is the marriage ever consummated.

1768: King Ferdinand I of Naples is married to Queen
Caroline. When Ferdinand is asked on the morning after
his wedding night how he likes his new bride, he replies:
"She sleeps like the dead and sweats like a pig."

1795: George, Prince of Wales (later King George IV) almost
faints when he first lays eyes on his wife-to-be, Princess
Caroline of Brünswick-Wolfenbüttel, the day before they
are due to be married. On their wedding night he gets
himself totally drunk in order to tolerate her "personal
nastiness" long enough to sleep with her once, after
which the two go their separate ways, never once
attempting to disguise their mutual loathing. When
Napoleon Bonaparte dies in 1821, a messenger rushes to
inform the king, "Your Majesty, your greatest enemy is
dead." George replies, "Is she, by God?"

1831: Emperor Ferdinand I of Austria marries seventeen-year-
old Princess Maria Anna of Sardinia. Thanks to centuries
of Habsburg royal inbreeding, Ferdinand is severely
physically and mentally handicapped and is both
epileptic and encephalitic. (His only recorded coherent
remark on any subject was "I am the Emperor, and I
want dumplings.") During the wedding night alone he
has five epileptic attacks: There are no children.

1846: Queen Isabel II of Spain is pressured into marrying her
first cousin Francis, the dwarfish homosexual duke of

Cadiz, although Isabel makes it clear that she finds her new husband repulsive. On the day of the wedding she gets blind drunk in order to face the ceremony. At the moment when they are pronounced man and wife, they burst into tears simultaneously. (When Isabel is asked years later about her wedding night, she replies, "What can I say about a man who wore even more lace than I did?")

1853: Leopold II, King of the Belgians, marries Queen Marie Henrietta, a teenage Habsburg duchess. Leopold is too ill to attend his own wedding and sends his brother-in-law, Archduke Charles, to stand in for him. Unfortunately for the sexually naïve Marie Henrietta, who had gone to her wedding bed armed only with instructions to submit to her husband's wishes, Leopold sufficiently recovers to attend the honeymoon. "If God hears my prayers," she tells a friend after her wedding night," I shall not go on living much longer."

History's
Ten Least Romantic
Honeymoons

1   Attila the Hun (406–53), King of the Huns, or "the
    Scourge of God" to his friends, was short, squat, and
    ugly; a Gothic historian described him as having "a large
    head, a swarthy complexion, small, deep-seated eyes, a
    flat nose, a few hairs in the place of a beard." He was
    also a regular ladies' man and had a dozen beautiful
    wives. On his wedding night with his twelfth, Ildico, one
    of his arteries burst and he died.

2   Eva Braun, married to boyfriend Adolf Hitler on April
    29, 1945, celebrated by swallowing poison the following
    day; the Führer took his own life two minutes later. On
    Hitler's orders, both bodies were cremated with gasoline
    in the Reich Chancellery garden.

3   The wedding night of Cesare Borgia, son of the
    sixteenth-century Pope Alexander, was wrecked when a
    practical joker switched his regular medication for a
    bottle of laxative pills.

4   At the age of twenty-eight, the famous Victorian author
    and art critic John Ruskin married his cousin Effie Gray,
    but on his wedding night he found the sight of his
    bride's pubic hair so distressing that they never shared a
    bed again. They spent a sexless honeymoon in Venice,
    where Ruskin painted, took notes on the local
    architecture, and mused on such higher matters as the
    decline of the Venetian empire. He later relented and
    promised to sleep with Effie again in three years' time,
    but he failed to keep his promise and the marriage was
    annulled.

57

5   George Albert Crossman and Ellen Sampson were
     married in January 1903, but on their wedding night had
     a marital tiff that resulted in the groom killing his bride
     by smashing her skull with a hammer. He hid the body
     in a tin box in an upstairs room at their home in Kensal
     Rise, London, where it remained for the next fifteen
     months until a lodger complained about the smells
     seeping into his room. When the police closed in,
     Crossman slit his throat with a razor.

6   John Harvey Kellogg, the inventor of the cornflake,
     spent his wedding night with Ella Eaton writing *Plain
     Facts for Old and Young*, a 644-page treatise on the evils
     of sexual intercourse. This included a ninety-seven-page
     essay, "Secret Vice (Solitary Vice or Self-Abuse)—Its
     Symptoms and Results," listing thirty-nine telltale signs
     indicating that someone was masturbating, including:
     "No. 7. Sleeplessness, No. 11. Love of solitude, No. 13.
     Unnatural boldness, No. 14. Confusion of ideas, No. 28.
     Use of tobacco, and No. 30. Acne." The marriage was
     never consummated.

7   In August 1994, Minnesota newlywed Gregory McCloud
     broke his back while carrying his 280-pound bride,
     Helen, over the threshold to their home. Doctors
     described the 140-pound groom's injuries as being
     consistent with those of someone who had been crushed
     by a car.

8   German bride Amy Weltz went to her wedding in
     Brisbane in September 1993 ignorant of the Australian

tradition of smearing wedding cake in the face of one's spouse. When her new husband Chas rubbed a slice of wedding cake in her face during the reception, she responded by smashing a bottle over his head, killing him almost instantly.

9   Japanese couple Sachi and Tomio Hidaki, married in 1978, did not get around to having sex for some time. The excitement of enjoying normal marital relations for the first time fourteen years later was too much for them and they both suffered fatal heart attacks.

10   According to Princess Diana's biographer Andrew Morton, as a special honeymoon treat, Prince Charles read her passages from the works of Carl Jung and Laurens van der Post.

In Delicato Flagranto Morto:
Five People Who Died During Sex

1 FELIX FAURÉ (1841–99), SIXTH PRESIDENT OF
THE FRENCH THIRD REPUBLIC On February 16,
1899 in the middle of the infamous Dreyfus crisis, Fauré
slipped away for a rendezvous with his mistress, Madame
Steinhal, wife of the artist Adolphe Steinhal. Legend has
it that Fauré's bodyguards heard a scream and broke
down the door to find him seated dead on a sofa with his
beautiful mistress kneeling in front of him *à la*
Lewinsky. According to some reports, she was in a state
of trauma-induced lockjaw and his member had to be
removed surgically. Madame Steinhal was thereafter
known as "the kiss of death."

2 LORD PALMERSTON, BRITISH PRIME
MINISTER (1855–58, 1859–65) "Old Pam," Britain's
horniest prime minister, died in his eighty-second year,
officially from pneumonia after catching a chill while
riding in his carriage; it was rumored, however, that he
had in fact died of a heart attack while engaged in a sex
act with a young parlor maid on his billiard table.

3 CARDINAL JEAN DANIELOU (1915–74) The
French have a phrase for orgasm—*le petite mort* (the
little death); in 1974, France woke to the news that one
of their most respected senior churchmen, a world-
leading Catholic theologian, the head of the theological
faculty at Paris University and the author of fourteen
books on sexual morality and church discipline had
experienced *le grand mort* when he dropped dead on the
stairs of a brothel in Clichy, the red-light district of
Paris. The French police explained that the seventy-year-

old Cardinal was on his way to "comfort" a twenty-four-year-old blond prostitute in an official capacity only.

4 NELSON ALDRICH ROCKEFELLER (1908–79)
A multimillionaire grandson of the oil magnate John D. Rockefeller, the forty-first vice president (to Gerald Ford) and the governor of New York, Rockefeller died in the saddle at the age of seventy-one while working on a late-Saturday-night "project" with his twenty-seven-year-old female research assistant. The unlucky researcher was pinned under her hefty boss's naked body for several minutes until she eventually phoned the paramedics. The *New York Times* noted that the larger-than-life septuagenarian Rockefeller "died the way he'd lived, with an enthusiasm for life in all its public and private passions."

5 POPE JOHN XII (C. 955–64) Known as John "the Bad," the pope was bludgeoned to death with a hammer by an irate husband who caught His Holiness in bed with his wife. When news of the death reached Rome, it was noted that Pope John was lucky to have died in bed, even if it wasn't his own.

Chapter Three

Courting the Muse

The Grim Rapper:
Ten Most Dangerous Bands in Popular Music

1   THE BYRDS Five members deceased: Gram Parsons (drug overdose, 1973), Clarence White (killed by drunk driver, 1973), Gene Clark (cardiac arrest, 1991), Michael Clarke (liver disease, 1993), John Guerin (cardiac arrest, 2004).

2   THE TEMPTATIONS Of their original five-man line-up of 1964–67, only one member, Otis Williams, survives. The others were Paul Williams (suicide shooting, 1973), David Ruffin (drug overdose, 1992), Eddie Kendricks (lung cancer, 1992), and Melvin Franklin (brain seizure, 1995).

3   THE GRATEFUL DEAD Four members deceased: leader Jerry Garcia (heart attack, 1995), Ron "Pigpen" McKernan (liver disease, 1973), Keith Godchaux (car accident, 1980), and Brent Mydland (overdose, 1990).

4   THE NEW YORK DOLLS Four members deceased: Bill Murcia (overdose, 1972), Johnny Thunders (overdose, 1991), Jerry Nolan (stroke, 1992), and Arthur Kane (leukemia, 2004).

5   T REX Four members deceased: Marc Bolan (car crash, 1977), Steve Currie (car crash, 1981), Steve Peregrine Took (cocktail cherry, 1990), and Mickey Finn (natural causes, 2003).

6   LYNYRD SKYNYRD Four members deceased: Ronnie Van Zant and Steve Gaines (air crash, 1977), Allen Collins (respiratory failure, 1990), and Leon Wilkeson (liver failure, 2001).

7   THE PLATTERS Four members deceased: David
     Lynch (cancer, 1981), Nate Nelson (heart disease, 1984),
     Paul Robi (cancer, 1989), and Tony Williams
     (emphysema, 1992).

8   ALLMAN BROTHERS BAND Three members
     deceased: Duane Allman (motorcycle accident, 1971),
     Berry Oakley (motorcycle accident, 1972), and Lamar
     Williams (cancer, 1983).

9   THE BEATLES Three members deceased: Stuart
     Sutcliffe (brain hemorrhage, 1962), John Lennon
     (murdered, 1980), and George Harrison (cancer, 2001).

10   THE RAMONES Three members deceased: Joey
     Ramone (lymphatic cancer, 2001), Dee Dee Ramone
     (heroin overdose, 2002), and Johnny Ramone (prostate
     cancer, 2004).

Last Curtain Calls:
Ten Showbiz Exits

1   1673: Overwhelmed by an unscripted coughing fit, the
French playwright and actor Molière collapses during the
fourth performance of his newly written *Le Malade
Imaginaire* and is carried to his home in the Rue de
Richelieu, Paris, where he dies. The play is about a
hypochondriac.

2   1870: The traveling James Robinson & Co. Circus and
Animal Show spices up its advance publicity for the
inhabitants of Middletown, Missouri, by having their
band perform on the roof of a cage full of Numidian
lions as the circus parades through the streets. Ignoring
repeated warnings that the cage roof is insecure and the
trick is highly dangerous, the show's managers order the
band to sit on it anyway. Sure enough, the roof gives way
and the musicians are thrown into the cage of hungry
lions below. Crowds look on as the lions tear legs and
arms from sockets, and half-devoured, dismembered
parts of the band are strewn across the cage floor. Of the
ten band members, three are killed outright and four
more are fatally mutilated.

3   1882: U.S. stage actress Annie von Behren stars in the
Coliseum Theatre, Cincinnati, in the drama *Si Slocum*, in
which her real-life fiancé Frank Frayne is required to
shoot an apple from her head with his back to her by
pointing the rifle over his shoulder. An audience of 2,300
watches as the bullet hits her neatly in the forehead. She
dies fifteen minutes later as the audience files out of the
theater.

4   1937: Publicity-seeking Norfolk vicar Reverend Harold
     "Jumbo" Davidson appears at Skegness Zoo, reading the
     Bible from a cage he shares with a large but normally
     docile lion called Freddie. The dramatic stunt goes awry
     when the lion turns on the vicar and mauls him. The
     audience, thinking it is a comic interlude, roars with
     laughter. As Davidson lies fatally wounded in the
     hospital, the show promoter erects banners inviting
     people to witness "the lion that injured the rector."

5   1943: During a regular live radio debate with four others
     about Adolf Hitler, Alexander Woollcott, author, critic,
     and radio personality, suffers a fatal cardiac arrest.
     Unaware that anything is wrong, hundreds of listeners
     phone in to complain that Woollcott, usually known for
     his stinging wit, has less to say for himself than usual.

6   1951: Ronald Reagan's finest moments on the silver
     screen, in *Bedtime for Bonzo*, are marred by the
     accidental death of his costar chimpanzee the day before
     the film's premiere.

7   1980: The Indian religious mystic Khadeshwari Baba
     attempts to demonstrate his powers of meditation by
     remaining buried alive in a ten-foot-deep pit for ten days.
     In a carnival-like atmosphere, a crowd of more than one
     thousand people, including several officials from the
     town of Gorakhpur, watch as Baba is ceremoniously
     lowered into the pit and the hole is filled in behind him.
     Ten days later, the pit is reopened. From the

accompanying stench it was estimated that Khadeshwari had been dead for at least a week.

8   1994: The Mexican entertainer Ramon Barrero, player of "the world's smallest harmonica," inhales and accidentally chokes to death on his mouth organ in mid-performance.

9   1996: Richard Versalle, a tenor performing at the New York Metropolitan Opera House, suffers a heart attack and falls ten feet from a ladder to the stage after singing the line "You can only live so long" from the opening scene of *The Makropulos Case*. It is a Czech opera about an elixir that confers eternal youth.

10   2004: Al Dvorin, the longtime announcer at Elvis Presley concerts, who coined the phrase "Elvis has left the building," dies in a car crash in California. He was on his way home from a convention of Elvis impersonators.

Fifteen Artistic Eccentricities

1   Friedrich von Schiller, the eighteenth-century German
    poet and dramatist, worked with his feet on a block of ice
    while inhaling the fumes of rotting apples.

2   The French poet Gérard de Nerval kept a pet lobster,
    which he took for walks around Paris on the end of a
    length of ribbon. He said the lobster was "quiet and
    serious, knew the secrets of the sea, and did not bark."

3   Jonathan Swift, after completing *Gulliver's Travels*, wrote
    a treatise on excrement in 1733 titled *Human Ordure*
    under the pen name Dr. Shit.

4   The Belgian-French pulp-fiction writer Georges
    Simenon, creator of the pipe-smoking detective Inspector
    Maigret, was the world's hardest-working author. Typing
    at a rate of eighty pages each day, Simenon wrote well
    over 400 novels. He said he found the strain of writing so
    extreme that it frequently caused him to vomit and made
    it essential for him to sleep with one or more women as
    soon as each book was done. Alfred Hitchcock phoned
    one day, to be told by Simenon's secretary that he
    couldn't be disturbed because he had just begun a new
    novel. Hitchcock, knowing that Simenon was capable of
    writing three novels a month, replied, "That's all right,
    I'll wait."

5   James Whistler, American-born painter and graphic
    artist, once dyed a rice pudding green so that it wouldn't
    clash with the walls of his dining room.

6   The opera composer Giacomo Mayerbeer, who lived in
    constant fear of premature burial, arranged to have bells

tied to his extremities so that any movement in his coffin would make a noise. So far, Mayerbeer has continued to decompose quietly without any sign of life.

7   Robert Louis Stevenson, the Scottish author of classic adventure yarns including *Treasure Island* and *Kidnapped*, spent his early years reading parts of the Bible aloud to sheep.

8   The German composer Robert Schumann had two imaginary friends called Florestan and Eusebius who gave him ideas for his scores. Schumann died in an insane asylum.

9   In 1863, the author Louisa May Alcott got sick and described in her journal how she suffered from terrible hallucinations in which she was repeatedly molested by a big Spaniard with soft hands. She recovered and went on to write *Little Women*.

10   The prolific nineteenth-century French writer Honoré de Balzac believed that sex was a drain on his creativity. After several months of abstinence, he was once tempted into a Paris brothel; he lamented afterward, "I lost a novel this morning."

11   Samuel Johnson wrote *Rasselas* in seven days flat to pay for his mother's funeral.

12   Arnold Bennett's novels were renowned for their stunning attention to detail. Bennett was complimented on his description of the death of Darius Clayhanger in the Clayhanger series, a death scene acclaimed as the

most realistic of its kind in the history of English literature. He explained his secret: While his father was dying he was at the bedside busy taking notes.

13   The eighteenth-century artist Benjamin West had an executed criminal exhumed and crucified to see how he hung.

14   Gustav Mahler, famous for his funeral marches, suffered from depression, hemorrhoids, and a morbid fixation on death: He wrote his first funeral march when he was six. Noticing that many other great composers, including Beethoven and Schubert, lived only long enough to compose nine symphonies, Mahler thought it was unlucky to write any more. He thought he could cheat death by calling his ninth great symphonic work a "Song Cycle" rather than a symphony. As soon as he had sketched out the first draft, however, he died suddenly of a streptococcal throat infection.

15   W. B. Yeats was in the habit of trying to hypnotize hens.

Killing Me Softly:
Ten Musical Moments

1968: The chairman of the People's Republic of China, Mao Zedong, bans the popular musical *The Sound of Music*, describing it as "a blatant example of capitalist pornography."

1975: During Christmas celebrations, the president of Equatorial Guinea, Macias Nguema, orders his army to shoot 150 political opponents in the Malabo football stadium as loudspeakers played Mary Hopkins's "Those Were the Days."

1978: Pop producer Phil Spector, a perfectionist in the recording studio, holds a gun to the head of Leonard Cohen to achieve the precise vocal performance he is looking for on his album *Death of a Ladies' Man*.

1992: Five prison guards at the Boise, Idaho, Maximum Security Institution are accused of taunting death-row inmates by playing the Neil Young song "The Needle and the Damage Done" during an execution by lethal injection.

1993: A Christian radio station in Vevay, Indiana, is burgled and set ablaze. Police say their prime suspect is a caller who became irate when a DJ refused to play "Don't Take the Girl" by Tim McGraw.

1994: In England, Dudley and District Hospital Radio ban the Frank Sinatra standard "My Way" from their airwaves because the lines "Now the end is near / And so I face the final curtain" are considered too discouraging for terminally ill patients. Other records suggested for the hospital danger list include Tony Bennett's "I Left My Heart in San Francisco" (insensitive to coronary patients) and Andy Fairweather-Low's "Wide Eyed and Legless" (unsuitable for amputees).

1994: A Beatles tribute band loses its "George Harrison" in a tragic highway accident. The "quiet Beatle," aka twenty-seven-year-old Duncan Bloomfield, falls out of the back of the band's van on the highway while they travel home from a performance in London. The rest of the band drives for twenty-five miles before they realize that he is missing.

1995: In Wanganui, New Zealand, a twenty-one-year-old man claims he has a bomb and takes over the local radio station, STAR FM, demanding to hear the song "Rainbow Connection" by Kermit the Frog.

1996: Mourners at a funeral service at All Saints, Gravesend, England, are startled when the church PA system inadvertently relays Rod Stewart's hit "Da Ya Think I'm Sexy," including the line "If you want my body."

1996: An academic report called *The Effect of Country Music on Suicide* by two American sociologists, Steven Stack and Jim Gundlach, proves a link between country music and losing the will to live. The study concludes that wherever country music is played, the suicide rate among whites is higher than average, "independent of divorce, Southernness, poverty, and gun availability."

Shock of the New:
Ten Great Moments in Art

1951: An abstract painting called "Autumn Landscape" by Scottish artist William Gear wins a prize at the Festival of Britain but is later denounced by the *Daily Mail* as a "jam pot thrown at canvas." In the House of Commons, Conservative MP Alan Gomme-Duncan announces the end of civilization as we know it.

1961: Piero Manzoni, a leading light of the art movement *arte povera*, exhibits a series of one-ounce cans containing his own excrement, titled "Artist's Shit." In June 2002, the Tate Gallery in London announces that it has purchased a tin of Manzoni's feces for about $38,000.

1966: Hermann Nitsch, Austrian "action artist," guts a dead lamb in London while showing a film about male genitalia. The *Times of London* calls the event a "brothel of the intellect." The organizers are prosecuted and fined.

1971: American artist Newton Harrison stages an exhibition at the Hayward Gallery, London, called "Portable Fish Farm," in which he plans to electrocute sixty live catfish. The show is canceled when comedian Spike Milligan makes his feelings known by lobbing a brick through the Hayward Gallery window.

1989: French/American sculptor Louise Bourgeois, whose work mostly features severed penises and huge testicles hanging singly or in pairs or bunches, exhibits a piece called "No Exit"—a stairway with two huge testicles restricting egress at the bottom—and one called

"Untitled (with Foot)" in which a baby is crushed by a large testicle.

1989: Canadian sculptor Richard Gibson is tried at the Old Bailey in London and found guilty of "outraging public decency" by creating earrings from freeze-dried human fetuses. They formed part of "Human Earrings," a mannequin head with wig. Gibson is fined $900, but the case costs $360,000 to prosecute.

1994: Christian Lemmerz, Danish artist, puts six dead pigs in a glass case so that visitors to the Esbjerg gallery can watch them change color from piggy-pink to black, via various shades of blue and gray. The artist declares it a triumph for people who value reality in art. The gallery owners declare it a triumph over their old ventilation system, which was unable to cope with the stench.

1995: Gilbert and George, British artists, display sixteen large glossy photos of themselves surrounded by a series of "defecation motifs," including turd circles and turd sculptures, which they call "Naked Shit Pictures," at the South London Art Gallery. A critic describes the work as "almost biblical."

1998: Californian performance artist Zhang Huan takes off his clothes, smears himself with pureed hot dog and flour, then allows himself to be licked by eight dogs at San Francisco's Asian art museum. Zhang says his aim is to "explore the physical and psychological effects of human violence in modern society." The exploration ceases when one of the dogs bites him on the bottom.

2005: Argentinean artist Nicola Constantino exhibits sculptures
made out of her own fat, which was removed during
liposuction. Four and a half pounds of the fat are
transformed to two sculptures of the female naked body,
which are offered for $460 each. Neither has been sold.

Entertainment and the F-Word:
Ten Great Moments

1965: British drama critic Kenneth Tynan, in the course of a live late-night talk show, becomes the first man ever to say "fuck" on TV, when he inquires, "What exactly is wrong with the word 'fuck'?" One hundred thirty-three shocked members of the House of Commons table four motions condemning him, and a Conservative member of Parliament insists that the fucker should be hanged.

1967: Michael Winner's film *I'll Never Forget What's'isname* features Mick Jagger's convent-educated girlfriend Marianne Faithfull saying the line, "Get out of here, you fucking bastard."

1970: Robert Altman's movie *M*A*S*H*, about the lives of triage doctors on the front lines of the Korean War, becomes the first Hollywood film to dare to use the F-word, although it was never in the original script.

1976: UK punk combo the Sex Pistols and a gang of suitably safety-pinned hangers-on are invited to appear on a prime-time UK TV show, *Tonight*. Presenter Bill Grundy, who hopes to inject some tension into a hitherto dull interview, quips, "You've got another ten seconds, say something outrageous." Guitarist Steve Jones takes up the challenge, noting that Grundy is a "dirty bastard," a "dirty fucker," and a "fucking rotter." A nation is scandalized and Grundy loses his job.

1983: Brian de Palma's film *Scarface* employs the F-word a record-breaking 206 times. In one scene, Tony Montana's girlfriend asks him, "Can't you stop saying 'fuck' all the time?"

1993: During the live televised Wimbledon tennis championships, the world's top male tennis player, "nice" Pete Sampras, is heard by photographers to admonish the center-court crowd, "Take that, you motherfuckers!"

1995: Martin Scorsese sets a new world record when his film *Casino* employs "fuck" 442 times—2.4 times per minute on average.

2003: At the Golden Globe Awards, U2 front man Bono describes the gong awarded for "The Hands that Built America" from the soundtrack of the film *Gangs of New York* as "really, really fucking brilliant." *Rolling Stone* magazine reports that, in response, eleven Republicans have sponsored a resolution demanding that broadcast regulators revoke the licenses of television stations that repeatedly air "indecent material." Meanwhile, a bill proposed by Congressmen Doug Ose and Lamar Smith aims to completely ban from all radio and network television broadcasts the words "shit," "piss," "fuck," "cunt," "cocksucker," "motherfucker," and "asshole."

2004: Elton John, exchanging pleasantries with his host during a live morning radio show, says "fuck." As the interviewer apologizes to his listeners, the veteran rock star asks if it is permissible to say the words "wank," "tits," "bugger," and "bollocks."

2005: At the Live8 concert in London, in front of an estimated live worldwide TV audience of 3.5 billion people, rapper Snoop Dogg invites the crowd to join in by putting their "motherfuckin' hands in the air."

T_em Rock & Roll Suicides

1.   SISTER LUC-GABRIELLE, NÉE JEAN DECKERS, AKA THE SINGING NUN A Belgian nun with an acoustic guitar provided the unexpected smash hit of 1963, "Dominique." She left her convent to discover the swinging sixties, but her new career flopped and, facing bankruptcy, she took her own life by carbon monoxide poisoning in a double-suicide pact with her lesbian lover.

2.   JOE MEEK, '60S RECORD PRODUCER OF THE TORNADOS Meek was unhealthily fixated on his idol, Buddy Holly. On the eighth anniversary of Holly's death, Meek shot his elderly landlady, then turned the gun on himself.

3.   DEL SHANNON, U.S. DOO-WOP IDOL He recorded "Hats Off to Larry" before blowing his own hat off with a .22-caliber rifle.

4.   IAN CURTIS, TWENTY-THREE-YEAR-OLD SINGER WITH THE BRITISH BAND JOY DIVISION He hanged himself in his kitchen on the eve of their first big U.S. tour.

5.   JOHN RITCHIE, AKA SID VICIOUS The Sex Pistols bassist failed in two suicide bids while in police custody for allegedly stabbing to death his girlfriend Nancy Spungen, but successfully overdosed on heroin as soon as he was released on bail in February 1979.

6.   PAUL WILLIAMS, A SINGER WITH THE TEMPTATIONS Williams was found dead in the street,

having shot himself a few blocks away from the Tamla Motown hit factory where he made his name.

7   RICHARD MANUEL, A MEMBER OF THE BAND Manuel cast a cloud over the group's important 1986 reunion tour by hanging himself in a motel room.

8   BOBBY BLOOM An American one-hit wonder whose cultural contribution "Montego Bay" was a hit in 1970, Bloom shot himself at the age of twenty-eight.

9   KURT COBAIN In April 1994, the twenty-seven-year-old Nirvana singer, who wrote a song called "I Hate Myself and I Want to Die," escaped from a detoxification center in Los Angeles, then shot his own face off. At the funeral service his wife, Courtney Love, read extracts from his suicide note. Days later, a sixteen-year-old girl in Turkey shot herself in a "tribute" to Kurt.

10   JEFF BUCKLEY The singer-guitarist drowned himself in 1997 in the Wolf River, near Memphis, Tennessee. Buckley, who is said to have had a Led Zeppelin fixation, was heard singing "Whole Lotta Love" as he swam into the river.

T𝑒𝑛 Creative Drunks

1   ERNEST HEMINGWAY The Nobel Prize–winning
    writer and adventurer had an epic appetite for alcohol
    and women. As a war correspondent during World War
    II, Hemingway acquired a special alcohol ration and
    positioned himself on a bar stool in the Paris Ritz,
    conducting his affairs between Bloody Marys. He kept
    drinking despite a severe liver problem, but it was a self-
    inflicted gunshot wound that finished him off at his
    Idaho retreat at the age of fifty-nine.

2   RAYMOND CHANDLER Chandler took to crime-
    writing after losing his regular job through drunkenness
    and absenteeism. He spent most of his adulthood in a
    drunken haze. In the words of his hard-drinking fictional
    detective, Philip Marlowe, "Alcohol is like love. The first
    kiss is magic, the second is intimate, the third is routine.
    After that you take the girl's clothes off." Unlike
    Marlowe, Chandler was a troublesome inebriate who
    suffered blackouts, fell over, threatened suicide, and
    generally irritated his friends. Chandler's devotion to his
    infirm wife Cissy kept him on the wagon for a while, but
    when she died in 1954, he hit the bottle and stuck to it,
    his health deteriorating rapidly. He died of pneumonia
    five years later.

3   JAMES BOSWELL His friend and mentor Samuel
    Johnson once advised him that "not to drink wine is a
    great deduction from life." Boswell took his advice to
    heart, partly to relieve frequent bouts of depression and
    partly to stimulate his appetite for prostitutes, a "whoring
    rage" that led to nineteen venereal infections. After one

82

of several drunken falls, Boswell remarked in his diary, "No man is more easily hurt with wine than I am." He finally finished *The Life of Samuel Johnson* in 1791, between bouts of heavy drinking, and died four years later of kidney failure at the age of fifty-five.

4   DOROTHY PARKER Her poisonous reviews as drama critic in *Vanity Fair* cost her her job, but her reputation as the wittiest woman in the country gave her a permanent place at the famous hard-drinking "round table" at New York's Algonquin Hotel. She often arrived at Algonquin lunches with a hangover that she insisted "ought to be in the Smithsonian under glass." "Last night I was so drunk," she told her friends, "I fell down and missed the floor." Her husband was similarly alcoholic and they were childless; a friend noted that she wouldn't "have anything in common with children because they don't drink." After four failed suicide attempts, she died at seventy-four when her liver gave way.

5   F. SCOTT FITZGERALD Said to write better drunk than most novelists could sober, he and wife Zelda lived a riotous lifestyle through the jazz age, their partying supplemented by the phenomenal success of *The Great Gatsby*. Unlike his more accomplished drinking companion, Ernest Hemingway, Fitzgerald was an abusive drunk with a habit of embarrassing himself in expensive restaurants by throwing ashtrays before passing out. Fitzgerald wrote presciently in the first draft of an autobiography: "Drunk at twenty, wrecked at

thirty, dead at forty." He wasn't far from the mark: He went into terminal decline—ill, drunk, and unable to recreate his early commercial success—and died of a heart attack in 1940, aged forty-four.

6   EDGAR ALLAN POE The self-destructive poet and short-story writer was an impulsive binge drinker and probably a laudanum addict, although it didn't stop him from joining the local temperance society and giving lectures on the evils of drink. Poe attended West Point Military Academy but was expelled for "gross neglect of duty" after appearing on parade naked except for a white belt and gloves. No writer of Poe's talent ever died lonelier or more pathetically. In 1849, he left home to visit friends in New York but never made it: After a mysterious five-day absence, he was found dying in a Baltimore gutter suffering from delirium tremens.

7   JACKSON POLLOCK The original "piss artist." Pollock was almost permanently inebriated from the age of fifteen, which explained the frequent fights he got into and his habit of relieving himself in public— although his incontinence occasionally came in handy, especially the time he set fire to his mattress and saved his life by urinating on it. It was rumored that Pollock would urinate on a canvas before delivering it to a dealer or client he didn't like, which gives his habit of naming his paintings "number one" and "number two" new meaning. Pollock went on the wagon for three years from 1948 to 1951, during which time he created his best-known Abstract Expressionist works, but sudden stardom

caused him to lapse, and he hit the bottle again. In 1956, his wife Lee Krasner left him, and a month later Pollock was killed after driving his car into a tree, killing one other passenger.

8   DYLAN THOMAS Reveling in his romantic image of the drunken poet, Thomas was often prone to exaggerating his own considerable drinking prowess. He liked to boast that he suffered from cirrhosis of the liver—a claim his autopsy eventually disproved. When he was drunk, Thomas was either a fantastic wit or a disgraceful bore, depending on your point of view. One evening he suddenly stopped in mid-flow and observed: "Somebody's boring me. I think it's me." On his final trip to New York, he began drinking very heavily and was unable to stop throwing up during a rehearsal of *Under Milk Wood*. He died at the age of thirty-nine while taking advantage of the long drinking hours in New York before starting a lecture tour. On November 9, 1953, he staggered out of a bar and fell into a fatal coma: His last words were "Seventeen whiskies—a record, I think."

9   BRENDAN BEHAN The greatest Irish playwright of his era described himself as "a drinker with a writing problem." Raised on whiskey by his maternal grandmother because it was "good for the worms," Behan achieved public notoriety with a series of drunken public appearances, including a memorable live TV interview during which he didn't manage to speak a single comprehensible word. Behan was once hired to write an advertising slogan for Guinness and was given

half a dozen kegs of their product for inspiration. After a month the company asked the legendary writer what he had come up with. Behan replied: "Guinness makes you drunk." He collapsed in a Dublin bar in March 1964 and died a few days later, aged forty-one.

10   GEORGE JONES Jones is said to have the best voice in the history of recorded country music. The tribulations of his booze-fueled third marriage to fellow country legend Tammy Wynette was detailed in various duets, from "We Can Make It" in 1971 through "We're Gonna Hold On" in 1974. In an attempt to wean him off liquor Wynette hid his car keys, making Jones a house prisoner. Desperate for a drink, he set off for Nashville in the only vehicle he could find keys for, his sit-down lawnmower. He was apprehended on the freeway. Jones was later twice convicted of drunk driving in Nashville, once following a televised police chase through the streets in 1983, then again after wrapping his car around a bridge in 1999.

T*en* Hard Acts to Follow

1   Ozzy Osbourne, no stranger to shock tactics, surpassed himself on January 20, 1982, during a gig in Des Moines, Iowa, when a fan threw a live bat onstage and Ozzy picked it up and bit its head off, believing it to be a rubber toy. Ozzy underwent a course of rabies injections. In May 1981, bored at a record-company press conference in Los Angeles, he repeated the trick by biting the head off a live white dove.

2   Tommy Minnock, a variety artist who plied his trade in Trenton, New Jersey, in the 1890s, allowed himself to be literally crucified onstage. As the nails were being driven into his hands and feet, Minnock sang "After the Ball Is Over."

3   The American entertainer Orville Stamm, by way of an encore, lay on his back with a piano on his chest, belting out "Ireland Must Be Heaven Because Mother Comes from There" while a pianist bounced up and down on his thighs.

4   The original cast of *Friends* had a seventh regular member, Marcel the monkey. He was fired because of his habit of vomiting live worms on the set.

5   In 1996, Dora Oberling, a stripper from Tampa, Florida, cheated death when a dissatisfied member of the audience tried to shoot her. The bullet bounced off one of her silicone breast implants.

6   Matthew Buchinger, a German living in the late seventeenth century, was the first all-round entertainer.

He mastered a dozen musical instruments and was a fine dancer and a brilliant magician. He was also an excellent marksman, a superb bowler, and an accomplished calligrapher. His chief claim to fame, however, was that he was 2' 4" tall and possessed neither arms nor legs.

7   In September 1994, a glass eye worn by Armando Botelli shattered when a soprano hit a high note during an opera in Milan.

8   Frenchman Joseph Pujol, the virtuoso of the anal accordion, earned fame and fortune at the turn of the nineteenth century as Le Pétomane. While lying in the bath, Pujol made the remarkable discovery that he could modulate sound with completely odorless farting. Pujol took his "act" to Paris, where he became an overnight sensation, outselling even France's favorite actress, Sarah Bernhardt. His performances included a series of imitations, such as the sound of calico being torn, a cannon, an eight-day-old pup, a creaking door, an owl, a duck, a swarm of bees, a bullfrog, and a pig. He could intone, by placing a small flute in his rectum, "By the Light of the Moon," and he could anally extinguish a candle at a distance of one foot. For an encore, Pujol inserted a yard of rubber hose with a cigarette in one end into his rectum, then drew on the cigarette and exhaled smoke. The highlight of Pujol's spectacular career was a continental tour that drew many of the crowned heads of Europe, although King Leopold II of Belgium felt obliged to see the show in disguise. When Pujol died in 1945, aged eighty-eight, he was succeeded by several

imitators, including a female "pétomane" called La Mere
Alexandre, who could imitate the farts of the famous and
perform a series of entertaining "occupational farts"
including those of nuns and freemasons. Her magnum
opus, however, was her impression of the bombardment
of Port Arthur. In the 1980s, an American "pétomane"
known as Honeysuckle Divine could extinguish a candle
flame at two paces and fart "Jingle Bells."

9   At the Organization of African Unity summit meeting in
       1975, Ugandan leader Idi Amin entertained his fellow
       African presidents by demonstrating how to suffocate
       people with a handkerchief.

10   The actor Lorne Greene had one of his nipples bitten off
       by an alligator while filming *Lorne Greene's Wild
       Kingdom.*

Essential Elvis Trivia:
The Top Ten

1   Before he discovered Elvis, Colonel Tom Parker's most notable success was "Colonel Parker's Dancing Chickens," an act that involved persuading chickens to perform by placing them on an electric hotplate.

2   There are an estimated 85,000 Elvis impersonators worldwide. In the Islamic city of Mogadishu in Somalia it is illegal to impersonate Elvis without a beard.

3   Elvis once ate nothing but meat loaf, mashed potatoes, and tomatoes for two years.

4   Elvis became addicted to Feen-a-mint chewing gum while attempting to overcome severe constipation.

5   Dr. Jukka Ammondt, a Finnish professor, is the only Elvis impersonator known to sing his songs in Latin, including "Nunc Hic Aut Numquam" ("It's Now or Never").

6   Next to sex and gluttony, the King's favorite nocturnal pastime was visiting the Memphis morgue to look at the corpses. He also liked to watch lesbian sex through a see-through mirror from his bedroom while nibbling on a bucket of giblets.

7   Elvis was once injected with the urine of a pregnant woman as part of a fad diet.

8   In July 1993, Air Force major Bill Smith, a Texan, filed a lawsuit in Fort Worth against the estate of Elvis Presley. Major Smith charged that Presley's estate had perpetrated a fraud by keeping up the pretense that the King had died in 1977. The major complained that this

had interfered with his attempts to sell his new book on Elvis's current whereabouts.

9   Elvis's last meal was four scoops of ice cream and six chocolate-chip cookies.

10   Death was Elvis's best-ever career move. If he had lived, he would have almost certainly been bankrupt within six months. In 2006, his estate, including the famous Graceland mansion, was estimated to be worth $150 million.

T*en* Notable Literary Deaths

1   1156: Pietro Aretino, an Italian satirist, poet, and critic, laughs so hard at a scene in a play involving one of his sisters that he falls off his chair, fatally striking his head on the floor.

2   1824: George Gordon (Lord Byron) catches a virulent form of rheumatic fever while rowing an open boat across a lagoon in a thunderstorm, in Greece.

3   1850: Honoré de Balzac dies of caffeine poisoning after regularly drinking about fifty cups of black coffee per day.

4   1867: Charles Baudelaire dies insane, paralyzed, and speechless at the age of forty-six from the combined effects of syphilis and addiction to alcohol, hashish, and opium.

5   1900: Oscar Wilde dies in France under the assumed name of Sebastian Melmoth from an abscess on the brain, which had spread from an infected middle ear, despite an operation by an ear specialist. When Wilde is told how much the failed operation had cost, he replied, "Oh, well then, I suppose I shall have to die beyond my means." (According to an even wittier but apocryphal version, Wilde's last words were "Either that wallpaper goes or I do.")

6   1915: Rupert Brooke, who wrote, "If I should die, think this only of me: 'that there's some corner of a foreign field / That is for ever England'," expires on a French hospital ship from blood poisoning, the result of an infected mosquito bite aggravated by sunstroke.

7   1931: Arnold Bennett is taken by typhoid, after cheerfully drinking a glass of tap water in a Paris hotel to demonstrate how completely safe it is.

8   1950: George Bernard Shaw falls out of the apple tree he was pruning at the age of ninety-four.

9   1963: Sylvia Plath, American poet, gasses herself in her kitchen oven at the age of thirty.

10   1983: Tennessee Williams chokes to death on a bottle cap that accidentally dropped into his mouth while he was using a nasal spray.

T*en* Thoughts on Shakespeare

1   VOLTAIRE "This enormous dunghill."

2   LEO TOLSTOY "Crude, immoral, vulgar, and senseless."

3   J. R. R. TOLKIEN "I went to King Edward's School and spent most of my time learning Latin and Greek; but I also learned English literature—except Shakespeare, which I disliked cordially . . ."

4   GEORGE BERNARD SHAW "With the single exception of Homer, there is no eminent writer, not even Sir Walter Scott, whom I despise so entirely as I despise Shakespeare when I measure my mind against his. It would be positively a relief to me to dig him up and throw stones at him."

5   WALTER SAVAGE LANDOR, BRITISH POET "The sonnets are hot and pothery, there is much condensation, little delicacy, like raspberry jam without cream, without crust, without bread."

6   DR. SAMUEL JOHNSON "Shakespeare never had six lines together without a fault. Perhaps you may find seven, but this does not refute my general assertion."

7   ROBERT GREENE, ENGLISH PLAYWRIGHT "An upstart now beautified with our feathers."

8   CHARLES DARWIN "I have tried lately to read Shakespeare and found it so intolerably dull that it nauseated me."

9   SAMUEL PEPYS "... and then to the King's Theatre, where we saw Midsummer Night's Dream, which I had never seen before, nor shall ever again, for it is the most insipid ridiculous play that ever I saw in my life."

10   KING GEORGE III "Is this not sad stuff, what what?"

Ten Hollywood
Suicide Shootings

1.   BOBBY HARRON The twenty-seven-year-old silent-movie star shot himself while depressed after being overlooked for the lead in *Way Down East* in 1920.

2.   KARL DANE The silent-movie star, overlooked when "talkies" arrived and no one could understand his heavy Danish accent, went home and shot himself in 1932.

3.   HERMAN BING The comic actor, six years after providing the voice-over for the Ringmaster in *Dumbo*, despondent over his fading career, shot himself in 1948.

4.   GEORGE REEVES In 1959, the original TV Superman, typecast and depressed over his inability to land another role, shot himself in the head in the upstairs bedroom of his Beverly Hills home while a party was in progress in the living room below. It was widely rumored that he believed he had acquired super powers and accidentally killed himself trying to fly.

5.   PEDRO ARMENDÁRIZ In 1963, the actor shot himself two weeks after working on *From Russia with Love*.

6.   GIG YOUNG Two years after receiving an Oscar for his supporting role in *They Shoot Horses, Don't They?*, he shot his wife and himself in a suicide pact three weeks after their wedding day in 1971.

7.   FREDDIE PRINZE The comedian and star of *Chico and the Man* shot himself in front of his manager after a messy divorce in 1977. The verdict of suicide was later altered to reflect an "accidental shooting due to influence

of Quaaludes," despite his suicide note: "I must end it. There's no hope left. I'll be at peace. No one had anything to do with this. My decision totally."

8   DONALD "RED" BARRY B-Western cowboy star who, despite a role in *Little House on the Prairie*, shot himself in 1980 because his fans had deserted him.

9   JON-ERIK HEXUM Committed accidental suicide in 1984 when he shot himself with a pistol loaded with blanks on the set of the TV spy show *Cover Up*, noting, "Let's see if this will do it." The concussion forced a chunk of his skull into his brain; he died six days later.

10   HERVÉ VILLECHAIZE The diminutive *Fantasy Island* star brought his life to an end by shooting himself in the stomach in 1993. He muffled the gun under two pillows so as not to disturb his sleeping girlfriend.

T𝑒𝑛 Literary Drug Abusers

1   CHARLES BAUDELAIRE Hashish and opium addict.

2   W. B. YEATS Addicted to mescaline, a hallucinogenic derived from Mexican cactus.

3   SAMUEL TAYLOR COLERIDGE Opium and laudanum addict.

4   THOMAS DE QUINCEY Opium and laudanum addict. The author of *Confessions of an Opium Eater* quaffed up to eight thousand drops of opium and six or seven glasses of laudanum a day. He started taking drugs for a toothache he suffered while at Oxford University. The remedy worked—eventually, all his teeth fell out and he had to live on liquids.

5   SIR ARTHUR CONAN DOYLE Cocaine user. He also had his most famous character, Sherlock Holmes, use it in *The Sign of Four*.

6   ROBERT LOUIS STEVENSON Cocaine addict. *Dr. Jekyll and Mr. Hyde* was created entirely under the influence of cocaine, which helped him write and twice revise the 60,000-word manuscript in six days.

7   CHARLES DICKENS Opium user.

8   ARTHUR RIMBAUD Absinthe addict.

9   DANTE GABRIEL ROSSETTI Morphine addict and alcoholic.

10   HUNTER S. THOMPSON, THE CREATOR OF "GONZO JOURNALISM" Renowned for excessive alcohol, heroin, and cocaine abuse.

Pennies from Heaven:
The World's Ten Highest-
Earning Dead Artists

1   Elvis Presley, the King of Royalties—$45 million per year

2   Charles Shulz—$28 million per year

3   John Lennon—$20 million per year

4   Andy Warhol—$16 million per year

5   Theodor S. Geisel (Dr. Seuss)—$10 million per year

6   Marlon Brando—$11.3 million per year

7   Marilyn Monroe—$8 million per year

8   J. R. R. Tolkien—$8 million per year

9   George Harrison—$7 million per year

10   Johnny Cash—$7 million per year

Chapter
Four

Health & Beauty

T*en* Presidential Illnesses

1   GEORGE WASHINGTON During his first year in
office, he developed a huge, pus-filled carbuncle that
made him seriously ill. Shortly afterward he caught a
cold in Boston, the start of a minor epidemic of what his
enemies called "Washington Influenza." In May 1790 he
almost died from pneumonia, causing him to reflect that
one more serious illness would surely "put me to sleep
with my fathers." Despite his pessimism, death did not
come until 1799, two years after his retirement from the
presidency. He rode around his plantation in the rain,
complained of a sore throat, and by the following
evening had suffocated to death, his airway blocked by a
swollen epiglottis. Washington, who had a morbid fear of
premature burial, had left instructions that he was to be
laid out for three days just to be on the safe side.

2   WILLIAM HENRY HARRISON He caught a severe
cold while giving his two-hour inaugural speech on a wet
day in 1841, and within days of taking office was
seriously ill with pneumonia and "congestion of the
liver," finally expiring four weeks later. Most people
blamed it on poor White House heating; however, *Globe*
editor Francis Preston Blair, not allowing the death of a
president to interrupt his assault on the administration,
blamed it on the Whigs, who had never before held the
presidency.

3   ZACHARY TAYLOR Became sick while attending
Independence Day ceremonies in sweltering heat at the
Washington Monument on July 4 and died suddenly a
few days later. The cause of death was disputed.

Officially listed as gastroenteritis (inflammation of the stomach and intestines), the cause is generally believed to be that Taylor ate cherries tainted with typhoid. Conspiracy theorists maintained that the president had been assassinated, probably by arsenic poisoning. This was disproved 141 years after his death when his remains were exhumed and samples of hair and fingernail tissue showed no trace of arsenic.

4   ABRAHAM LINCOLN Lincoln probably suffered from Marfan's syndrome, which could account for his extreme lankiness and disproportionately long limbs. He also suffered from regular bouts of serious depression, variously ascribed to a hereditary disposition (his mother and sister both suffered from "melancholia"), a bang on the head after falling from a horse, and syphilis. Shortly after delivering the Gettysburg Address, Lincoln got sick and was covered with red blotches. His doctor diagnosed a mild form of smallpox and informed him that the disease was highly contagious. Lincoln replied: "Now I have something I can give everybody."

5   GROVER CLEVELAND A heavy smoker, he had a large cancerous growth on his upper palate—on his "cigar-chewing side"—a condition kept so secret that even his vice president didn't know about it. In 1893, Cleveland underwent a risky operation aboard his yacht, kept secret from the public, the press, and the Cabinet. The evident problem with the president's mouth was later explained as a "severe toothache."

6   WOODROW WILSON In the middle of a lecture tour in 1919, he suffered a major stroke, resulting in brain damage and paralysis, turning his trademark radiant smile into a frightening leer. The White House effected a massive cover-up as Wilson lay seriously ill and incapacitated for seven months, during which time twenty-eight bills were passed without the president's signature. Wilson's illness was kept a secret from the Cabinet and even the vice president and from the American public, who learned about it only years after his death.

7   FRANKLIN D. ROOSEVELT He suffered a severe attack of poliomyelitis when he was thirty-nine years old, resulting in total paralysis of both legs to the hips. His condition led to the biggest public deception in the history of presidential illnesses, pulled off with the full cooperation of the press. Newsreels never showed him being wheeled or carried, and of the 35,000 photographs of Roosevelt in the presidential library, only two show him in a wheelchair. While campaigning for his fourth term in August 1944, to dispel rumors of failing health, he gave a speech standing up with the aid of leg braces. The effort involved made him ill, and he complained of pains in the back of his head. FDR died unexpectedly on April 12, 1945, less than six months after being elected to a fourth term in office.

8   DWIGHT D. EISENHOWER He had a major heart attack that required emergency treatment just eighteen

months into his presidency in 1955, but he broke with precedent by releasing information about his illness to the public, although most of what the public learned was carefully screened. Nine months later, a serious bowel obstruction caused him to have another tricky operation—a procedure his surgeons were reluctant to perform, given his recent heart problems. In November 1957, with three years of his second term in office remaining, he suffered a stroke that seriously affected his speech, but he returned to work after just three days.

9   JOHN F. KENNEDY Winning a presidential campaign based almost entirely on his alleged youthful vigor, he suffered from a variety of afflictions, including Addison's disease, a deficiency of the adrenal glands. It was treated with a type of steroid associated with psychiatric side effects including depression, mania, confusion, and disorientation. He also had back problems so severe that he could not pick up his son; this was treated with highly suspect injections from Max "Dr. Feelgood" Jacobson. Nine years after Kennedy's death, Jacobson was barred from practicing medicine after being found guilty of forty-eight counts of professional misconduct, mostly involving the illegal prescription of amphetamines to patients.

10   LYNDON B. JOHNSON Underwent a major operation to remove his gallbladder and a stone from his ureter. Unknown to the public and the press, Johnson had a history of heart trouble and had developed a dangerously accelerated heartbeat while undergoing anesthesia. To

allay suspicions, the White House press secretary bluffed his way through the president's convalescence by putting out film of Lady Bird Johnson planting a tree outside the hospital room window and the president himself watching *Hello Dolly!* on television. The recovering Johnson was eager to discuss the heroic job his doctors had done. While holding a press conference in the Bethesda Naval Hospital grounds, he suddenly whipped up his pajama top to reveal a twelve-inch scar under his right ribs, noting, "Those fellows had to go through thirty-four feet of intestine." It wasn't the first time Johnson chose this method to illustrate a medical point; he once dropped his trousers at a White House reception to show off a hernia repair.

Foul Play:
Ten Great Sporting Scandals

A.D. 67: Roman chariot racers doped themselves and their
horses with mysterious herbal infusions, including a
solution of dried boar's dung to promote muscle
growth, in the search for speed. Emperor Nero out-
cheats them all when he competes in the A.D. 67
Olympic Games and bribes judges to declare him
chariot champion despite the fact that he had fallen
out and failed to finish the race.

1900: Supervision of the early Olympic marathons was a
trifle lax. The winner of the 1900 event in Paris, an
enterprising local baker's delivery boy named Michel
Theato, used his knowledge of the city geography to
take advantage of a few shortcuts down back alleys and
side streets. Four years later at the St. Louis Olympics,
the marathon was held on a grueling course on a hot
afternoon, and only fourteen of the original thirty-two
starters made it to the finish, led by an uncannily
fresh-looking American, Fred Lorz. He was just about
to accept his gold medal on the winner's podium when
word got around that he had hitched a lift from a
passing motorist who had dropped him just outside the
stadium after conveying him the last eleven miles.
Controversially, his gold medal went to Thomas Hicks,
whose trainers had given him a mixture of brandy and
strychnine to keep him going.

1904: The Tour de France reaches an all-time low amid
widespread skullduggery and outright cheating.
Spectators leave nails in the road in front of their
favorites' rivals, while riders take car trips and even

108

train rides. The first four riders are disqualified, including one who had been pulled along by the car in front by means of a wire attached to a cork in his mouth. Although he finishes three hours behind the first-place rider and with two flat tires, race officials declare Henri Cornet the winner.

1919: Disbelieving American sports fans discover that everything has its price when eight members of the Chicago White Sox, one of the most talented but worst-paid teams in baseball history, are charged with taking a bribe to throw the World Series against the Cincinnati Reds. When the trial begins in 1921, most of the records from the grand jury including the records of the players' testimony have "disappeared." The trial lasts for several weeks, but the jury eventually finds all eight not guilty. However, "Shoeless" Joe Jackson and seven accomplices— pitchers Eddie Cicotte and Claude "Lefty" Williams, third baseman George "Buck" Weaver, first baseman Arnold "Chick" Gandil, utility man Fred McMullin, shortstop Charles "Swede" Risberg, and centerfielder Oscar "Happy" Felsch—are banned from professional baseball for life.

1932: Stella Walsh dominates the Olympic 100-meter sprint, confirming her status as the top female sprinter of the 1930s. Forty-three years later, after becoming an American citizen and being inducted into the U.S. Track and Field Hall of Fame, she is killed by a stray bullet in a Cleveland robbery. The autopsy reveals that "she" is a he. Ironically, when Walsh lost her title in Berlin in 1936 to her bitter rival Helen Stephens, her teammates hinted that Stephens was too fast to be a woman. (Doctors examined the new champion and confirmed that she was female.) Four years later, another Olympic gender-bender, Hitler Youth member Hermann Ratjen, dreams of glory for the Fatherland when he tapes up his genitalia and enters the Berlin Olympics as "Dora." Disappointingly, he just misses out on the medals when he finishes in fourth place in the women's high jump.

1972:   Sports' most inventive cheat may have been Boris Onischenko, a Red Army major from Ukraine. A veteran of the modern pentathlon—a five-discipline event including fencing—Onischenko arrives at the Montreal Olympics as a hot favorite for the gold, having won two silvers and a bronze in three previous Olympiads. Britain's epée No. 1, Sergeant Jim Fox, is outclassed and easily outpointed by Onischenko, but complains that his opponent has been scoring without actually hitting anyone. Upon examination of the Soviet athlete's sword, it is revealed to be wired up so he can trigger the electronic scoring system with his hand and register a hit at will. "Boris the Cheat" exits the Olympics in disgrace as a new career in the Siberian salt mines beckons.

1964:   The track and field medals fly Moscow's way as the statuesque Soviet sisters Tamara and Irina Press add to their impressive haul of twenty-six world records and

110

five Olympic golds. Their bulging biceps, deep voices, and prominent Adam's apples raise eyebrows, however, and two years later, under pressure from America, gender testing is introduced for the first time. The Press sisters go into immediate retirement, allegedly to care for their sick mother.

1986:   With the score goalless in the 52nd minute of the 1986 World Cup quarterfinal soccer match between England and Argentina, the 5' 4" Argentinean Diego Maradona miraculously outjumps England's goalkeeper, Peter Shilton, who is almost a foot taller, to head the ball into the England net. Tunisian referee Ali Bennaceur is the only person in the stadium who has failed to notice that Maradona used his left hand to guide the ball home. "It was partly the hand of Maradona, partly the hand of God," the Argentine captain explains later. After this divine intervention, Argentina wins the game and goes on to win the World Cup.

1990:   Jockey Sylvester Carmouche emerges from thick fog at the Delta Downs racetrack in Vinton, Louisiana, to finish in first place on 23–1 long shot Landing Officer, a suspicious twenty-four lengths ahead of his nearest rival and barely a second outside the course record. Race officials become even more suspicious when they discover that none of the other jockeys can actually recall seeing Carmouche at all during the race. In fact, he had dropped out of the mile-long race and rejoined it just before the end. Carmouche protests his innocence but is handed a ten-year ban.

2000:   The intellectually disabled Spanish Paralympics
        basketball team storms to victory, beating Russia in the
        men's final. The euphoria of winning a gold medal is
        soon obliterated when it becomes clear that ten of the
        team's twelve members have no mental deficiency
        at all.

Ten Reliable Tudor Remedies

1   Asthma: Swallow young frogs or live spiders coated in butter.

2   Gout: Boil a red-haired dog in oil, then add worms and the marrow from pig bones; apply the mixture.

3   Headache: Rub the forehead with a rope used to hang a criminal.

4   Rheumatism: Wear the skin of a donkey.

5   Jaundice: Drink a pint of ale containing nine drowned head lice every morning for a week.

6   Bubonic plague: Hold a live chicken against the sores until the bird dies.

7   Whooping cough: Find a ferret, feed it with milk, then give the leftover milk to the sick child.

8   Warts: Lay half a mouse on the wart for half an hour and then bury it in the ground. As the mouse rots, the wart will vanish.

9   Baldness: Rub dog or horse urine into the scalp.

10   Deafness: Mix the gallstone of a hare and the grease of a fox, warm the result, and place it in the ear.

Read 'Em and Wipe: Twelve Magic Moments in Toilet Paper History

1400: The first toilet paper is made for the Emperor of China. It is available in one size 2'-by-3' sheets.

1509: King Henry VIII appoints a Groom of the Stool, whose sole function is to clean the royal anus by hand. It becomes a highly respected and coveted position.

1725: The French author François Rabelais, in his book *Gargantua*, recommends wiping with nettles, velvet, handkerchiefs, carpets, or, for added comfort, the neck of a goose.

1750: Mussel shells and corncobs are widely used for cleaning purposes. Hawaiian islanders, however, prefer to use coconut husks.

1880: Publishers of *The Old Farmer's Almanac* improve circulation by punching a hole in the corner of their respected organ so it can be hung on a nail in the outhouse.

1890: The Scott Paper Company manufactures the first perforated toilet roll, but is reluctant to put its name on its groundbreaking product. It is demurely described in their advertisements as "curl papers for hairdressing."

1930: Sears customers are enraged when their catalog, another popular outhouse choice, is produced on glossy, nonabsorbent paper.

1942: Britain's first soft two-ply toilet paper, advertised as "splinter-free," is available only from Harrods.

Meanwhile, the country's best-selling novelty toilet paper is single-ply printed with images of Adolf Hitler.

1967: During recording sessions for *Sergeant Pepper's Lonely Hearts Club Band*, Beatle George Harrison complains to EMI about the studio's hard, scratchy toilet paper. An executive decision is taken at boardroom level to replace it with the softer variety.

1984: A Christian group, the World Reformed Alliance, sends twenty thousand free Bibles to Romania, where dictator Nicolae Ceauşescu has promised to distribute them. The Bibles arrive, but Ceauşescu confiscates the lot and has them pulped to ease a national toilet paper shortage. The quality of Romanian pulping is so poor, however, that words such as "God" and "Jeremiah" are still clearly visible.

1994: A severe national toilet paper shortage in Cuba leads to the ransacking of a library, where rare books are stolen and torn apart. An official explains that most Cubans have long since used up their telephone books.

1999: Japanese inventors unveil the paperless toilet, a device that washes, rinses, and blow-dries the user's bottom with a heating element.

History's Ten Greatest Fashion Mistakes

1   SEE-THROUGH TOGAS *De rigueur* in Emperor
    Nero's Rome, these diaphanous garments, exposing both
    the breasts and the genitals, left nothing to the
    imagination. Complained the Roman philosopher Seneca,
    "Our women have nothing left to reveal to their lovers in
    the bedroom that they have not already shown on the
    street."

2   THE CODPIECE In 1482, King Edward IV introduced a
    law that forbade persons below the rank of lord to expose
    their private parts in public. The answer was the essential
    fashion accessory for Renaissance men, cut to fit snugly
    around the male member like the finger of a glove.
    Fifteenth-century fashion critics were not impressed.
    Michel de Montaigne sniffed, "What is the purpose of
    that monstrosity that we to this day have fixed to our
    trousers, and often which is worse, it is beyond its natural
    size, through falseness and imposture?"

3   EXPOSED GENITALS The best-dressed gentleman
    around medieval England exposed his naked genitals
    below a short-fitting tunic. If the genitals didn't hang
    low enough, a chap could wear padded flesh-colored
    falsies, called "braquettes."

4   FLEA CRAVATS These were designed to catch *Pulex
    irritans*, also called the human flea, and were worn for
    about two hundred years from the fourteenth century
    onward by Renaissance ladies. The furry human flea-
    collars were removed and shaken out to lessen the chance

of fleas coming into contact with the rest of their clothing.

5   FALSE EYEBROWS These became highly desirable among eighteenth-century men and women, who wore sets of eyebrows, cut from mouse skin and stuck on with fish glue, to make them appear fashionably surprised.

6   BOUND FEET According to one of several versions of the story, the Chinese fetish for foot-binding, designed literally to keep women in their place, dates from the thirteenth century with the Empress Taki, who was born with a clubfoot. Her courtiers took to binding their own feet in cloth in imitation, and soon small, tightly bound designer feet became highly desirable in Chinese women, even though bound toes were likely to become gangrenous. Chinese husbands, meanwhile, encouraged foot-binding because their crippled wives were less likely to run off. Foot-binding was officially abolished by Chairman Mao in 1949.

7   THE PRINCE ALBERT Queen Victoria's consort gave his name to a form of body piercing, once popular amongst Victorian gentlemen. In order to maintain a perfectly smooth trouser line of the tight trousers that were fashionable at the time, Albert allegedly wore a ring through his penis, which was then strapped to his thigh.

8   SOLIMAN'S WATER This was the sixteenth-century facelift, guaranteed to eliminate spots, freckles, and

warts. Unfortunately, the application of a blowtorch to your face would have had similar consequences, as the chief ingredient of this top-selling lotion was mercury, which burned away the outer layers of skin and corroded the flesh underneath. Another side effect was that teeth fell out even more quickly than was usual at the time.

9   HAIR REMOVAL BY IRRADIATION An indispensable item in the best North American beauty parlors in the 1920s was the recently invented X-ray machine, employed to remove unwanted facial and body hair. Other treatments available included radioactive face creams to lighten the skin and radioactive toothpaste for whiter teeth and better digestion, after which the customer could enjoy a radium-laced chocolate bar. As recently as 1953, a company in Denver was promoting a radium-based contraceptive jelly.

10   COLORED TEETH Sixteenth-century Italian ladies colored their teeth red or green. Russian women, however, always dyed theirs black.

Twelve Phobias

1   Apotemnophobia—fear of amputees

2   Bolshephobia—fear of Bolsheviks

3   Bromidrosiphobia (or bromidrophobia)—fear of body odor

4   Defecaloesiophobia—fear of painful bowel movements

5   Eurotophobia—fear of female genitalia

6   Geniophobia—fear of chins

7   Medomalacuphobia—fear of losing an erection

8   Papaphobia—fear of the pope

9   Peladophobia—fear of bald people

10 Taeniophobia—fear of tapeworms

11 Venustraphobia—fear of beautiful women

12 Zemmiphobia—fear of the great mole rat

T*en* Phobias of the Famous

1   Augustus Caesar, King Henry III of France, Napoleon
    Bonaparte, Benito Mussolini, Adolf Hitler: aliurophobia
    (fear of cats)

2   Harriet Martineau, Edmund Yates, Wilkie Collins, and
    Giacomo Mayerbeer: taphophobia (fear of premature
    burial). The writer Harriet Martineau left her doctor $35
    with instructions that he should make sure she was well
    and truly deceased before her burial by cutting her head
    off. The novelist Edmund Yates similarly left a fee for
    any surgeon kind enough to slit his jugular vein before
    interment. The novelist Wilkie Collins always carried a
    letter with him imploring anyone finding him "dead" to
    contact the nearest doctor for a second opinion.

3   Brad Pitt: ichthyophobia (fear of sharks, even on dry
    land).

4   Nicolae Ceauşescu, Benito Mussolini, Marlene Dietrich:
    bacillophobia (fear of germs). The Romanian dictator
    Ceauşescu and his wife Elena went on staged
    "walkabouts" which required them to shake a few hands
    and kiss small children. The secret police selected a few
    volunteers beforehand and had them locked up for weeks
    and regularly disinfected in readiness for the big day.
    Mussolini adopted the Roman-style straight-arm fascist
    salute because he couldn't bear the idea of shaking hands
    with people. Marlene Dietrich's obsession with germs led
    her to be known by Hollywood insiders as "the Queen of
    Ajax."

5   Alfred Hitchcock: ovophobia (fear of eggs).

6   Frederick the Great, Natalie Wood: hydrophobia (fear of water). The king of Prussia was so terrified of water that he could not wash himself and his servants had to rub him down with dry towels. Natalie Wood fell off a yacht and drowned in 1981.

7   George Bernard Shaw: coitophobia (fear of sex). Shaw lost his virginity to a much older woman at the age of twenty-nine. He was so shocked by the experience that he didn't bother to try it again for another fifteen years.

8   Maximilian Robespierre: hematophobia (fear of blood). The French revolutionary kept the guillotine in the Place de la Revolution in Paris in almost continuous use. Robespierre himself, however, was extremely squeamish and couldn't bring himself to even look at the bloodstains on the street cobbles.

9   Robert Schumann, German composer: metallophobia (fear of metal). He especially disliked keys. (But not, apparently, the key of E-flat major, in which he wrote his Symphony No. 3.)

10   Queen Christina of Sweden—entomophobia (fear of insects). The mentally unbalanced seventeenth-century monarch had a miniature four-inch cannon built in perfect working order so that she could spend most of her time firing tiny cannonballs at the fleas in her bedroom.

The Wonder of You:
Ten Facts about
the Human Condition

1. The human body comprises enough fat to make seven bars of soap, enough iron to make a medium-sized nail, enough potassium to explode a toy cannon, enough lime to whitewash a small chicken house, enough sugar to fill a jam jar, and enough sulfur to rid a dog of fleas.

2. A complete skeleton is worth between $5,000 and $7,500 to a medical student; your skull alone would fetch only about $450.

3. Your mouth produces about one quart of saliva per day.

4. *Demodox folliculorum* has eight stumpy legs and a tail, is about a third of millimeter long, and loves nothing more than to recline in the warm, oily pits of your hair follicles. Most adults have this mite, usually on the head and especially in eyelashes, and often in nipples.

5. You have approximately 4,000 wax glands in each ear.

6. The average adult stool weighs about four ounces. About half of the bulk of your feces comprises the dead bodies of bacteria that live inside your intestines.

7. The average male foot exudes half a pint of sweat each day.

8. If it weren't for the slimy mucous that clings to and lines the walls of your gut, your stomach would readily digest itself.

9. The average person will pass about 11,000 gallons of urine in a lifetime.

10. A man weighing 200 pounds would provide enough meat to feed 100 cannibals in one sitting.

Twelve Historic Operations

1658: Thomas Hollier, a London surgeon specializing in lithotomy, removes a bladder stone "as big as a tennis ball" from the young Samuel Pepys. The diarist recovers, but complains afterward that he often passes "gravel" in his urine, which he tries to cure by drinking turpentine.

1667: A pioneer attempt at blood transfusion is made as members of the Royal Society in England, unaware that blood-type compatibility is important, gather to witness the transfusion of twelve ounces of sheep's blood into the unfortunate Reverend Arthur Coga. Samuel Pepys, still sore from his encounter with Thomas Hollier (see above), records in his diary: "The patient speaks well, saying that he finds himself much better, as a new man . . . but he is cracked a little in his head." Reverend Coga dies soon afterward.

1686: King Louis XIV of France undergoes an operation for anal fistulas. Twice he is sliced open without any form of anesthetic, but the word from the palace of Versailles is that he endured the operation heroically. A group of French nuns at the cloister of Saint-Cyr hear of his recovery and celebrate by writing a song called "Dieu Sauvez le Roi." A traveling Englishman hears the tune, copies it down, and when he gets home translates it into "God Save the King."

1745: Proving that the only two qualifications for a good surgeon that matter are fast hands and an iron stomach, royal surgeon William Cheselden arms his assistant with a watch and removes a kidney stone in under sixty seconds, but throws up after the operation.

1797: Admiral Horatio Nelson has his right arm amputated, without anesthetic, on board the *Theseus* on July 25. Nelson is so upset by the feel of the cold scalpel against his flesh that he orders that all amputations performed on ships under his command should be done with warm knives. After the arm is removed he is left alone to recover with an opium pill and a shot of rum, the start of a lifelong opium addiction.

1805: Napoleon's head surgeon, Dominique Larrey, sets a new record by amputating a leg in less than fifteen seconds.

1821: King George IV has a sebaceous cyst removed from his head, entirely without the aid of anesthetic, and casually asks the surgeon, Astley Cooper, "So, what do you call these tumors?" As mark of the patient's gratitude, plain Astley became Sir Astley.

1842: The Scottish surgeon and part-time body snatcher Robert Lister, described as "the finest surgeon in Europe," sets a personal best for a leg amputation at twenty-eight seconds. While achieving this record, he accidentally cuts off two of his assistant's fingers and the patient's left testicle.

1846: The first amputation carried out under anesthetic is performed at Massachusetts General Hospital when twenty-one-year-old Alice Mohan is parted from her right leg. The operation is performed by Dr. George

Haywood, assisted by Andrew Morton and his new invention, the ether inhaler. When the young woman regains consciousness, Haywood, understandably pleased with his efforts, plucks the leg from the sawdust where it lies and waves it triumphantly under her nose, saying, "It's all done, Alice." There is no record of her reply.

1846: The famous English engineer Isambard Kingdom Brunel accidentally swallows a gold half-sovereign, which sticks in his windpipe. After vomit-inducing drugs fail to dislodge it, surgeons try unsuccessfully to remove the coin via a tracheotomy. The coin is finally expelled by a more basic method: The engineer has himself strapped to a hinged table, tilted to a 45-degree angle, then thumped hard in the back. Much to Brunel's relief the coin shoots forward and hits his teeth.

1881: President James Garfield, shot by the assassin Charles Guiteau, is attended by the first of sixteen doctors, Willard Bliss, who jabs a finger into the wound, then inserts a nonsterile probe to find the bullet. Bliss fails to find the slug, but he does so much damage with his probe that it misleads everyone into concluding that the missile had penetrated the president's liver and therefore surgery is useless. An army surgeon general sticks his unwashed finger into the wound, followed by the navy surgeon general who probes with his finger so deeply that he punctures the president's liver. Alexander Graham Bell is called in with a metal detector to locate the offending missile and, after several passes, Bell announces that he has located the bullet. Doctors decide to cut Garfield open to remove it. What Bell's equipment had actually located, however, is the metal spring under the mattress; the bullet remains undetected. The deep and by now infected wound causes Garfield to have a fatal heart attack. The president's autopsy confirms that the bullet had lodged some way from the spine and that Garfield would have survived if the doctors had only left him alone.

1887: Queen Victoria has a particularly nasty axillary abscess drained at the age of fifty-one. When she comes around from the chloroform, she opens her eyes and remarks, "A most unpleasant task, Professor Lister, most pleasantly performed," once again proving that royal patients are not only a lot braver than the rest of us when they have to go under the scalpel, but that their breeding makes them far more courteous.

Ten Health Problems That Helped Napoleon Meet His Waterloo

1 Nausea

2 Pituitary dysplasia

3 Prolapsed hemorrhoids

4 Constipation

5 Syphilis

6 Chronic fatigue

7 Peptic ulcer

8 Dysuria (difficult or painful urination)

9 Abdominal cramps

10 Anorexia

Of Lice and Men:
Ten Great Unwashed

1   SAINT FRANCIS OF ASSISI St. Francis listed personal filthiness among the insignia of piety, in line with the early teachings of the Christian Church, which held that dirtiness was next to godliness and that bathing was an evil, ungodly vanity punishable by an eternity in hell. One fourth-century Christian pilgrim boasted that she hadn't washed her face for eighteen years. St. Anthony never washed his feet, St. Abraham didn't wash his hands or feet for fifty years, and St. Sylvia never washed any part of her body except her fingertips.

2   LUDWIG VAN BEETHOVEN The German composer had such a disregard for personal cleanliness that his friends had to take away his dirty clothes and wash them while he slept.

3   CHAIRMAN MAO The Chinese Communist leader never took a bath or brushed his teeth—the latter on the grounds that tigers never brushed their teeth either. He achieved an epic personal hygiene problem that grew steadily worse as the years went by; the septuagenarian having several young concubines rub his body down with hot towels, instead of bathing.

4   RAMASUBBA SITHARANJAN The Bombay religious mystic eschewed personal hygiene as proof of his faith to his followers and claimed to have not brushed his teeth, bathed, or shaved in sixty-five years.

5   CZAR PETER THE GREAT Renowned throughout Europe for his lack of personal hygiene, he was

incredibly smelly even by eighteenth-century standards and was blissfully unaware of rudimentary table manners or even basic potty training. When the Czar and his courtiers visited London, onlookers noted that they intermittently dripped pearls and lice as they walked.

6   KING FREDERICK THE GREAT His clothes remained unchanged for years and he shuffled in rags around his palace, which was, in places, ankle-deep in excrement provided by his pack of beloved Italian greyhounds. When he died, the shirt on his back was so rotten with sweat that his valet had to dress him in one of his own shirts for the burial.

7   KING LOUIS XIV The king was an enthusiastic lover, but his advances were a trying time for his mistresses. When his doctor persuaded him to bathe for medical reasons, the French king tried to get out of it by feigning a terrible headache and vowed never to repeat the experience. He took only three baths in his lifetime, each of them under protest.

8   GENGHIS KHAN The Mongol ruler's warriors were a superstitious bunch who believed that washing was a sacrilege. There was also a more practical reason for the lax approach to ablutions: The thick crust of dirt that covered their bodies throughout their lives helped them withstand temperatures as low as minus 43° F. Khan's men used their lack of hygiene as a weapon of psychological warfare: Their enemies could smell the

festering Mongol hordes long before they could see them, and were often paralyzed with fear by the time they arrived.

9   THE ELEVENTH DUKE OF NORFOLK Renowned as one of the richest and smelliest men in England, the "Dirty Duke" never once voluntarily bathed in his entire life: When his servants found it impossible to occupy the same room with him, they got their aristocrat employer blind drunk and quickly bathed him before he regained consciousness.

10   KING HENRI IV The French king was known, unusually for the time, for being a stickler for changing his shirts regularly, but still went around his court "smelling like carrion." When his fiancée, Marie de Médicis, met him for the first time, the stench almost made her faint.

T*e*n Dangerous Doctors

1   GALEN The third-century Greek anatomist, personal
    physician to the Roman emperor Marcus Aurelius, killed
    more people than any other man in medical history. For
    more than one thousand years Galen was acknowledged
    by the Roman Catholic Church to be the world's only
    official authority on human anatomy. The Church was
    not in the least concerned that Galen had never actually
    seen the inside of the human body, or that his one
    hundred or so medical textbooks were wild guesswork
    based on his observations of dead pigs and dogs. Thanks
    to Galen, generations of medical students learned that
    the brain was a large clot of phlegm, that the heart had
    two chambers, that the best way to cure a headache was
    to cut holes in the skull, that the quickest way to cure a
    cough was to amputate the uvula at the back of the
    patient's palate, and that postoperative wounds should be
    dressed with pigeon's blood.

2   GUY FAGON The eighteenth-century resident French
    physician at the court at Versailles was known as "the
    killer of princes." Within fourteen days in 1715, he
    wiped out almost the entire French royal family by
    treating a measles epidemic with a tough regime of
    purges, emetics, and prolonged bleedings. The infant
    Louis XV survived only because his nurse refused to hand
    him over to Fagon and hid him. Fagon once advised King
    Louis XIV to drink nothing but Burgundy for his health.

3   DR. WALTER FREEMAN The professor of neurology
    at George Washington University invented the
    "production line lobotomy," performed with an ice pick

and a hammer under local anesthetic. Freeman's first patient was a sixty-three-year-old woman from Kansas, who had second thoughts upon learning that her curly blond hair would have to be completely shaved off. Freeman reassured her that she could keep her curls, confident that after the operation she would no longer care. In the 1940s and 1950s, the Freeman lobotomy was performed on more than twenty thousand patients as he toured the U.S. in his specially equipped camper van, his "Lobotomobile." His most famous patient was the rebellious Hollywood starlet Frances Farmer, who was subjected to the Freeman lobotomy at the age of just thirty-four; he even had a photo taken of himself performing it.

4   JOHN RICHARD BRINKLEY A small-town doctor working in Milford, Kansas, in the early 1900s, Brinkley believed that he could renew a man's sex drive by transplanting the sexual glands of a goat into the male scrotum. He persuaded a local farmer to allow him test his theory, and a year after his transplant the farmer's wife gave birth to a baby boy named "Billy." For a mere $750, Brinkley offered his services to anyone willing to undergo his surgery, and he found plenty of eager subjects. The first few transplants, using gonads from the odorless Toggenberg breed of goats, were performed without any major hitch. His goat-gland therapy came to the attention of Harry Chandler, owner of the *Los Angeles Times*, who also underwent Brinkley's surgery and publicized the technique in his newspaper. The

publicity made Brinkley famous, but with it also came
the unwanted attentions of the California state medical
authorities, who quickly revoked his license to practice
and began criminal proceedings. In the 1930s, Brinkley
hit upon a new radio scam, "Doctor Brinkley's Medical
Question Box." Listeners were invited to write to him
with their health problems and he would prescribe his
own treatments on the air. These cures invariably
involved his own product line of patent medicines, which
for the most part were colored water.

5   ROLANDO SANCHEZ Minutes before going into
surgery to have his gangrenous right foot amputated in
February 1995, the fifty-one-year-old diabetic William
King joked with the staff at the University Community
Hospital in Tampa, Florida, "Make sure you don't take
the wrong one." King awoke to discover that surgeon
Rolando Sanchez had inadvertently removed his left foot,
leaving the gangrenous foot intact. He subsequently had
both legs amputated below the knee and settled with the
surgeon for $250,000. Later, the hospital revealed that it
had implemented a new system to make sure that such a
ghastly accident could never be repeated: In the future,
the word "no" would be written in marker pen on all
limbs that were not to be amputated.

6   DR. THEODORE MORELL Morell was Adolf Hitler's
personal doctor from the mid-1930s onward. Hitler was
prone to temper tantrums that became worse as World
War II went on, prompting his subordinates to nickname
him "carpet biter." These mood swings were exacerbated

by a variety of minor ailments, including stomach
cramps and chronic insomnia, which Morell treated with
a regimen of twenty-eight separate medications,
including some mercury-lead compounds known to cause
mental deterioration, and Dr. Köster's anti-gas pills, a
mysterious mixture of strychnine and belladonna. Morell
also prescribed "golden" tablets containing huge
amounts of caffeine and the highly addictive
amphetamine pervitin, large doses of which are known
to cause disorientation, hallucinations, convulsions, and
coma. In September 1940, Hitler threatened to bomb
England with one thousand tons of explosives. He later
amended the figure to five tons because the original
quantity, arrived at under the influence of Morell's pills,
struck him as excessive on reflection. The physician who
replaced Morell, Dr. Geising, found that Hitler had been
cumulatively poisoned over a period of many years by a
variety of drugs in a "truly horrifying concentration."
Geising, however, was not entirely blameless: In 1944, he
treated a cold with a 10-percent cocaine solution, and in
Hitler's last days gave him large quantities of cocaine
drops for an eye complaint.

7   SIR WILLIAM ARBUTHNOT LANE This surgeon
of Guy's Hospital, London, was responsible for possibly
the most painfully misguided medical mistake of the
twentieth century, surgical removal of the colon. Lane's
life was dominated by two great passions, ballroom
dancing and the condition of the human bowel. The
latter, he believed, was the seat of all known medical

problems. Lane advised his patients to oil their colons daily with a pint of cream and to sleep flat on their stomachs, and made the remarkable claim that red-haired women were naturally immune to constipation. In 1903, he made the breakthrough "discovery" that the human colon was useless, merely an unnecessary tube of tissue and muscle full of nasty smells. Lane set about testing his hypothesis by ridding the world of colons. Patients who came to see him for minor ailments had their colons removed and tossed into the incinerator as a matter of routine. Before long his theory became fashionable and surgeons all over the world agreed that the humble colon was responsible for a whole range of diseases including cancer and tuberculosis. The fad lasted for about ten years before Lane's work was widely discredited.

8   SIR JAMES CLARKE Queen Victoria spent much of her reign in the hands of this mysteriously incompetent court physician, a man once described as "not fit to attend a sick cat." Clarke was involved in a court scandal when one of the queen's young unmarried ladies-in-waiting got sick with a swollen stomach, which convinced several people, including the queen herself, that she was pregnant. To prove her innocence, Miss Hastings agreed to a humiliating internal examination by the queen's doctor. Clarke reported that although he could not find evidence of pregnancy, he could see no other good reason for her swollen stomach. Then he produced a bizarre medical statement that concluded that

although the lady in waiting was still a virgin, that didn't
necessarily mean she was not pregnant: He had come
across a few cases in his time, he explained to the queen,
of pregnant virgins. The truth became evident a few
months later when the girl died in agony from a tumor
on her liver. Clarke's career should have been terminated,
but the queen retained his services, and when her
husband Prince Albert became ill in November 1861,
Dr. Clarke was on hand to assure both the prime minister
and the queen that Albert was suffering from no more
than a nasty cold and there was absolutely no need for
concern. Within six weeks the prince was dead.

9   EDWARD BODKIN In 1999, this fifty-six-year-old
resident of Huntingdon, Indiana, was arrested and
charged with performing unlicensed surgery after he had
removed the testicles of at least five men. He was about
to castrate a sixth when the patient panicked and handed
over to police a videotape Bodkin had lent him of some
of the operations. Most of the testicles were recovered
from several small jars in Bodkin's apartment, each
labeled with the dates of the procedures, the subjects'
initials, and either an "L" or an "R." Bodkin admitted
castrating his clients for free in exchange for the right to
videotape the operation, and to selling the films for $75
each. His discount gelding service improved with
practice; at first, he used an art knife, manicure scissors, a
curved needle, and rusty needle-nosed pliers, but by the
last castration, he was using surgical equipment
purchased from a veterinary supply company and an

anesthetic. When asked to comment on the patients' motives, state prosecutor John Branham said, "I can't sit here as a reasonable human being and give you an intelligent answer to that."

10   DR. HAROLD SHIPMAN A GP from Hyde, near Manchester, England, Shipman was sentenced in 2000 to fifteen life sentences for the murder of fifteen patients, fourteen female and one male, by diamorphine injection. An inquest later concluded that Shipman was probably responsible for as many as 297 suspicious deaths during the twenty-four years he practiced in Hyde, including eight patients in one street alone. His victims were mostly elderly, single women who gave Shipman the privacy he needed to administer lethal injections during home visits. No motive was ever offered for the murders, but psychiatric reports suggest that Shipman simply enjoyed watching people die. He was found hanged in his prison cell four years into his sentence. An inquest in 2005 attributed even more deaths to Shipman, carried out during his time as a junior doctor, bringing the estimated total of murders to about 350.

I Have a Little List:
Ten Deformities
of the Famous

1 MOSES A reluctant public speaker who described himself as "heavy of mouth," he had a major speech impediment and probably suffered from a cleft lip and palate. In Exodus 6:12, Moses describes himself as having "uncircumcised lips."

2 ANNE BOLEYN She had six fingers on her left hand and three nipples. If King Henry VIII's divorce petition had failed, he planned to use the extra digit and supernumerary nipple as evidence that she was a witch.

3 MARSHAL CHARLES MAURICE DE TALLEYRAND The French revolutionary and statesman had a deformed leg, the result of being dropped by his nurse.

4 KING RICHARD III He was the subject of a number of colorful inventions. According to one, he was born with a full set of teeth and with hair down to his waist. His famous hunchback was also probably invented by his enemies; no portrait, suit of armor, or contemporary description attests to it.

5 LORD BYRON The Romantic poet was born with a clubfoot, which he later attributed to his mother's tight corsets.

6 NAPOLEON The emperor had hemicryptorchidism— one undescended testicle.

7 KAISER WILHELM II His left arm was stunted and withered, the result of a complicated breech birth.

8   JOSEPH STALIN His left foot had webbed toes and his left arm was shorter than his right.

9   JOSEF GOEBBELS He was born with a left leg three inches longer than his right. According to the official version it was the result of a childhood illness; the possibility that one of the architects of the Nazi movement had a genetic defect didn't sit well with the prevailing ideology.

10   ADOLF HITLER According to Soviet medical reports, he did indeed have only one ball. According to Eva Braun, Hitler's testicular damage was the result of "a boyhood mishap" with a wild alpine goat.

T*e*n Bad Hair Days

1   Mary Queen of Scots was bald, a secret she hid from even her closest acquaintances with a thick auburn wig. The fact that Mary was follically challenged became horribly clear on the day of her execution. The executioner picked up her decapitated head by the hair to show it to the crowd and her wig came away in his hand.

2   In 1993, a twenty-two-year-old Dutchman went on a rampage that caused $60,000 damage to a barbershop in Hengelo. He was upset because the barber had overdone his request for "a slight trim."

3   In 1994, hundreds of Uruguayans sued a local shampoo manufacturer after using the patent dandruff treatment Dander-Ban. Within hours of using the shampoo they all became completely bald.

4   In March 1983, Danish hair-fetishist Luigi Longhi was jailed for life after he was found guilty of kidnapping and murdering a female German hitchhiker. Longhi admitted he'd washed her hair four times before strangling her.

5   In 1966, Michael Potkul won a $400,000 malpractice award against surgeon Dominic Brandy in Pittsburgh after Brandy promised Potkul a new head of hair. He achieved this by grabbing the hairy scalp at the back of Potkul's head and stretching it over the bald bit on top. Potkul became depressed after six unsuccessful operations to correct the problem and attempted suicide.

6   The composer Gioacchino Rossini suffered from alopecia in his later years, which made him completely bald. He took to wearing a wig; in exceptionally cold weather, however, he wore two or three wigs simultaneously.

7   In 1994, Ernestine and John Kujan sued the New York dog-grooming salon Pet Pavilion after watching their cocker spaniel Sandy accidentally bake to death in an automatic blow dryer.

8   In 1996, California hairdresser Joseph Middleton was sentenced to sixty days of community service. Middleton had masturbated with his free hand while doing a female customer's hair. At his trial, the court heard that he had been able to finish both jobs because the customer was too frightened to object.

9   The Albanian dictator Enver Hoxha banned beards and long hair, even on visiting foreigners. Albanian border barbers were employed to snip excess hair from all foreigners entering the country; the degree of hairiness was then noted in police files.

10   Henry Ford always washed his hair in water containing rusty razor blades, in the belief that rusty water was a hair restorer.

Twelve Milestones
in Oral Hygiene

350 B.C.: Hippocrates, the "father of medicine," recommends a toothpaste made of three mice and the head of a hare.

50 B.C.: Romans relieve toothache by tying toads to their jaws and make toothpastes and mouthwashes from urine; apparently the very best piss was Portuguese.

A.D. 50: The Greek scholar Pliny advises that toothache can be avoided by eating two mice a month and recommends "pervasive green frogs, burnt heel of ox, toads and worms" as a cure for halitosis.

1590: Elizabethans relieve toothache by applying sweat from the anus of a cat that had been chased across a plowed field. Queen Elizabeth I loses the last of her teeth and fills the holes in her mouth with cloth to improve her appearance in public, but somehow remains a virgin.

1768: A novel method of tooth extraction is perfected by Dr. Messenger Monsey, resident physician to the Chelsea Royal Hospital, London. He takes a strong piece of catgut, winds one end around his tooth, threads the other end through a specially prepared bullet with a hole drilled through it, loads the bullet into his revolver, and fires. Monsey complains that he finds it difficult to persuade his friends and patients to follow his example.

1770: A London dentist, Martin Van Butchell, promises "gums, sockets and palate formed, fitted, finished and fixed without drawing stumps or causing pain," a bold claim given that he is working in the pre-anesthetic age. His technique amounts to hitting a prospective patient over the head with a large stick, or blowing a trumpet in his ear seconds before a tooth is to be pulled.

1780: While spending time in a debtor's prison in London, an Englishman named William Addis carves a handle out of a cow's thighbone, bores holes into it, and attaches bristles of cow hair, creating an exciting new dental accessory, the toothbrush.

1865: Tons of teeth from the Civil War dead are shipped to England to be worn by the rich and the fashionable and to satisfy a craze for tooth transplants—a surgical procedure first performed by John Hunter in the 1750s. Although highly dangerous, the practice, which encourages poor people to sell their own perfectly good teeth, continues until shortly before World War I.

1880: Cheap celluloid dentures are invented by an English dentist who dislikes handling the teeth of dead men. They are briefly popular but never really catch on, as they are highly flammable and prone to spontaneous combustion if the user smoked.

1884: The first use of anesthesia by nitrous oxide— "laughing gas"—is made by Horace Wells, a young dentist living in Connecticut. Wells didn't live long enough to enjoy the full rewards of his marvelous discovery. The medical profession laughed, and Wells, haunted by ridicule, began sniffing chloroform. One day, in a chloroform-induced delirium, he ran into the street and doused two passing prostitutes with acid. Wells killed himself before his case came to trial; he smuggled a can of chloroform into his cell, opened a main artery, and bled painlessly to death.

1938: Chinese boar hairs, the favored material for toothbrush bristles, are replaced by nylon, which is considered a more hygienic substitute. Boar-hair bristles, although subject to bacterial growth, still account for 10 percent of toothbrush sales worldwide.

1995: Following the death of one of his patients, Stephen Cobble, a dentist from Tennessee, is charged with professional incompetence. Former patients complain that he has given them checkups by having his assistant rub their backs, stomachs, and arms; sedated them by administering injections to their groins and navels; transferred scar tissue from a cesarean section to treat a jaw disorder, made a patient stand with one foot on a stack of magazines, and prescribed a diet of beef, salt, eggs, and a quarter pound of butter daily.

T*en* Great Sporting Moments

A.D. 165: The Greek athlete Peregrinus set himself on fire during the Olympic Games to prove his faith in reincarnation. He hasn't reappeared at any subsequent Olympic meetings, although he did enjoy a small cult and his staff came to be regarded as a religious relic.

A.D. 850: The size of a regulation soccer ball, roughly the same as a man's head, is arrived at by design: English soldiers enjoy kicking around the head of a dead Danish brigand.

1649: The first grandstands are built around Tyburn Tree in London so that crowds of up to 100,000 can watch public hangings.

1862: During interludes in the Civil War, both armies pass the time by staging louse races.

1925: Frank Hayes becomes the first deceased person to win a steeplechase. Hayes rides a 20–1 outsider, Sweet Kiss, to victory at Belmont Park, but when the horse's owner and trainer go to congratulate him, they find him firmly attached to the saddle but slumped forward. Doctors confirm that a fatal heart attack made him an ex-jockey before he crossed the finish line.

1956: Chairman Mao's Physical Culture and Sports Commission recognizes a new track-and-field event, the hand-grenade throw.

1976:   At the Montreal Olympics, Princess Anne, a member
          of Great Britain's equestrian team, becomes the only
          female competitor allowed to forgo a routine sex test.

1978:   Sports newscaster Phil Rizzuto, in the middle of his
          commentary during a baseball game, is informed of
          the sudden death of Pope Paul VI. "Well now,"
          Rizzuto tells millions of baseball fans, "that kind of
          puts a damper on even a Yankee win."

1994:   Colombian soccer player Andres Escobar is gunned
          down by an irate wine waiter after scoring a goal
          against his own team—a mistake that helped
          eliminate his country from the World Cup
          tournament.

1996:   At Thailand's national pre-Olympic trials, the men's
          volleyball gold medal is won by a team of
          transsexuals from northern Lampang Province. To
          the great disappointment of the players, who have
          breasts but have yet to undergo genital surgery,
          none of them are selected for the Olympic team.

'Rhoid Rage:
Ten Hemorrhoid Sufferers

Socrates

Emperor Nero

Alexander the Great

Martin Luther

Lewis Carroll

Charles Dickens

Edgar Allan Poe

Percy Bysshe Shelley

Queen Victoria

Marilyn Monroe

Ten Cures No Longer Recommended by the Medical Profession

1   The Roman physician Pliny the Elder taught that human urine was an excellent remedy for dandruff, running sores, venereal disease, and mad-dog and snake bites.

2   In the Middle Ages, it was fashionable to eat, and to rub into the body, parts of ancient Egyptian mummies for medicinal purposes. The body parts of decomposing Egyptians were widely touted as a cure for abscesses, fractures, contusions, paralysis, migraine, epilepsy, sore throats, nausea, disorders of the liver and spleen, and internal ulcers. Mummy trafficking became a lucrative and highly organized business, starting in Egyptian tombs and following a well-planned route to Europe. The bottom finally fell out of the mummy market in the late seventeenth century, when people found out that dealers were selling "fake" mummy made from recently murdered slaves.

3   The most popular cure for leprosy in the Middle Ages was bathing in the blood of a dog. If a dog wasn't available, a two-year-old child's blood would do.

4   In the sixteenth century, most learned people were convinced of the magical medical properties of Bezoar stones—hard secretions often formed in cows' stomachs or goats' gallbladders. The groundbreaking French barber-surgeon Ambroise Paré offended many people, especially the French king, Charles IX, who was a big Bezoar fan, when he suggested that the stones were completely useless. Paré decided to set up an experiment to prove his point. A cook who had been convicted of

theft and sentenced to public strangulation was offered a choice between receiving his sentence, and swallowing a lethal poison along with a Bezoar stone, thought to be the perfect antidote. He chose the latter and died. King Charles concluded from this experiment that the cook's Bezoar stone had been a fake.

5   The seventeenth-century German surgeon Wilhelm Hilden advised the use of postoperative balm made from powdered mummy, earthworms, iron oxide, pig brains, and moss from the skull of a man who had been hanged under the sign of Venus. The truly innovative part of Hilden's prescription was that this mixture was to be applied not to the wound, but to the knife that caused it.

6   Early suggested cures for syphilis included having intercourse with a virgin, rubbing dung into the male organ, and bathing in horse urine. The only regular precaution taken to avoid venereal disease in Elizabethan times was to wash the genitals in vinegar. Eighteenth-century cures for venereal disease included a sound thrashing and having the penis wrapped in the warm parts of a freshly dismembered fowl.

7   Until the sixteenth century, when the French surgeon Ambroise Paré proved it unnecessary, the standard cure for male hernias was castration.

8   Britain's first prime minister, Sir Robert Walpole, ate about 180 pounds of soap over a period of several years in an attempt to get rid of a stone in his bladder.

149

9   The wealthy nineteenth-century politician and country squire Jack Mytton of Halston, Shropshire, died at age thirty-eight after sustaining injuries from setting fire to his own nightshirt in an attempt to cure his hiccups. Before the horribly burned Mytton expired, he remarked, "Well, the hiccups is gone, by God."

10   The nineteenth-century New York physician Dr. Thomas Spencer attempted to cure cholera by plugging the patient's anus with sealing wax.

Ten Celebrity Fashion and Beauty Tips

1   Chairman Mao's gray military-style "Mao suit," previously known as the Sun Yat-sen suit and later worn by millions, made its first appearance in 1949. Mao's chief of protocol, Yu Yinqing, suggested that in the future he stick to the more conventional dark suit when he was receiving foreign dignitaries. Yu's fashion tip went unheeded; he was fired and later committed suicide.

2   On the day of his execution, King Charles I wore two undershirts. It was very cold and he didn't want anyone to see him shivering.

3   When the wardrobe of Empress Josephine, first wife of Napoleon Bonaparte, was inventoried in 1809, she was found to own 666 winter dresses and 230 summer dresses but only two pairs of underpants.

4   Few in the diplomatic corps have served with as much distinction as Queen Anne's cousin, Lord Cornbury, the third Earl of Clarendon, who was the governor-general of New York and New Jersey from 1701 to 1708. The veteran British parliamentarian, a burly transvestite in his spare time, opened the New York Assembly wearing satin shoes, a blue silk ball gown studded with diamonds, and a fancy headdress. When Queen Anne's American subjects complained about their governor's dress, Cornbury dismissed the locals as "stupid." It was perfectly obvious, he said, that as a representative of Her Majesty he had a duty to represent her as accurately as he could. Queen Anne had him recalled.

5 In an attempt to make himself more attractive to his girlfriend Gala, Salvador Dalí shaved his armpits until they bled and wore a perfume made of fish glue and cow dung.

6 When syphilis robbed the great sixteenth-century Danish astronomer Tycho Brahe of his nose, he had an attractive artificial nose made of gold and silver.

7 The famous French racing driver Jean Behra wore a plastic right ear after losing the original in a racing crash in 1955. He always carried a spare in his pocket just in case.

8 George Washington had at least four sets of false teeth, which he soaked in port overnight to make them taste better. By the time he became president he had only one tooth left and used a set of dentures fashioned from cow's teeth. Washington later contacted a leading dentist in Philadelphia, who produced a state-of-the-art set carved not from wood, but from hippopotamus tusk. The new dentures were thoughtfully drilled with a hole to fit over Washington's remaining tooth. Unfortunately they were a very bad fit and the cause of constant pain, which the president tried to ease by taking laudanum. Washington is noted for not smiling very much for his portraits.

9 The Soviet leader Joseph Stalin was never seen without his high, heavy black riding boots, even on the most inappropriate occasions and uncomfortable conditions. He once had one of his bodyguards sent to the salt mines for

not wearing boots. It turned out that the bodyguard had taken to wearing slippers so as not to wake Stalin when he was sleeping. Stalin had him arrested for plotting to assassinate him. A guest once asked Stalin why he never took his boots off even on a stifling hot day. The Russian leader replied, "Because you can kick someone in the head with them so hard he'll never find all his teeth."

10   Mae West wore eight-inch platform shoes and false nipples.

Chapter Five

Crime & Punishment

Hard Ax to Follow:
Ten Famous Executioners

1   The chief executioners of Constantinople during the
    Ottoman Empire excelled in diverse methods of
    dispatching their victims, including drowning by slow
    degrees and forcing the victim to imbibe ground glass.
    The most active of them all, Souflikar, the executioner
    during the reign of Mahomet IV, preferred simple
    strangulation. He personally throttled about five
    thousand people over a period of five years.

2   The Duke of Alva, the chief executioner to King Philip
    of Spain, was hired for his efficiency in wiping out
    heretics during the Holy Inquisition. His chosen method
    of execution was to seal the victim's mouth with an iron
    gag that allowed only the tongue to protrude, then to
    brand the tongue with a hot iron so it became swollen
    and could not be withdrawn. The victim was eventually
    burned alive. At Antwerp, the duke executed eight
    thousand people in one session. King Philip passed the
    most ambitious death sentence of all time in 1568 when
    he declared that the entire population of the
    Netherlands—approximately 3 million people, was
    heretical and therefore should be executed. It was a
    tough nut to crack even for the Duke of Alva, although
    he did manage to kill 800 people during Holy Week.

3   Richard Brandon, son of the chief executioner Gregory
    Brandon, was destined to become England's most famous
    executioner. Known in the trade as "young Gregory," the
    boy put in hours of practice on his ax technique by
    decapitating cats and dogs and boasted that he never
    needed more than one blow of the ax to remove a

victim's head. The climax of his distinguished career was
the removal of King Charles I's head on January 30,
1649, although on that day Brandon was a reluctant
executioner—he and his assistant insisted on wearing
masks and false beards to avoid any possible
repercussions.

4   The innovative nineteenth-century English executioner
William Marwood invented the "modern" method of
hanging. Until Marwood's day, hanging usually involved
a very short drop and slow strangulation at the end of a
rope; the executioner often had to weight the victim by
wrapping himself around his legs. Recoveries from
hangings were commonplace. In 1871, Marwood
perfected the long drop, a system that caused the victim
to fall from six to ten feet through a trapdoor. The drop
fractured the neck's vertebrae, severing the spinal cord
and medulla and so causing instant death and reducing
the suffering of those hanged. Marwood didn't always get
it right; the long drop often resulted in accidental
decapitation.

5   London's eighteenth-century chief executioner, John
Thrift, was considered the most incompetent man ever to
have held that position. Thrift, a convicted murderer who
was set free on condition that he did the government's
dirty work as an axman, was unsuited to the job: He was
highly strung, unsure with the ax, and liable to burst into
tears at inappropriate moments. His biggest problem was
that he couldn't stand the sight of blood. When he was
called upon to execute the Jacobite rebel Lord Balmerino

at the Tower of London in 1745, he fainted, then lay on the ground sobbing while onlookers tried to persuade him to get on with it. When Thrift finally picked up his ax he took five blows to sever Balmerino's head. Thrift never quite got the hang of it, yet he somehow managed to blunder and hack his way through a seventeen-year career. He was hated by the public for his clumsiness, and when he died in 1752 a mob pelted his coffin and his pallbearers with stones and dead cats.

6   The best-known executioner of the French Revolution was Charles Henri-Sanson, the most competent member of an extraordinary family that served the nation with six generations of public executioners from 1635 to 1889. Sanson became so adept at his job, thanks to endless practice on the necks of French aristocrats, that he was able to dispatch twelve victims in thirteen minutes. At the height of the Reign of Terror he removed the heads of three hundred men and women in three days. His guillotine in the Place de la Revolution was so busy that residents in a nearby street complained that the stench of blood from the stones was a health hazard and lowered the value of their houses. On October 16, 1793, 200,000 people turned out to watch Marie Antoinette lose her head. They were all kept waiting while Henri-Sanson untied her hands so she could empty her bowels in a corner behind a wall before her head was cut off.

7   Italy's most celebrated executioner, Mastro Titta, plied his trade on behalf of the pope, carrying out 516 public executions from 1796 to 1864. Known for his casual

scaffold manner, Titta would occasionally offer the condemned person a pinch of snuff just before removing his or her head. His work clothes, still stained with the blood of his last job (carried out when he was eighty-five), are on display at the Rome Museum of Criminology.

8   Australian hangmen bore the official title Executioner and Flagellator, as they were also required to carry out whippings. Elijah Upjohn, who hanged Ned Kelly, was the country's most famous. Like most Australian hangmen, Upjohn was also a convicted felon, originally arrested for drunkenness, indecent exposure, defecating in a main street, and unnatural practices with a chicken. Fortunately for Kelly, his hanging was one of the few that Upjohn got right; he was usually drunk. It was still a very unpopular execution, and afterward Upjohn, harassed by the public, lost his nerve and was fired by the government.

9   Grover Cleveland, the only American president to serve two nonconsecutive terms, personally carried out the execution of two criminals. As sheriff in Buffalo, New York, in 1872 he hanged twenty-eight-year-old Patrick Morrissey, who had been convicted of stabbing his mother to death while drunk. Six months later he hanged twenty-nine-year-old murderer Jack Gaffney. When Cleveland ran for the presidency in 1884 his rivals called him the "Buffalo Hangman," but it didn't harm his candidacy.

10   Edwin T. Davis was the world's first official state
      electrocutioner. An electrician by trade, Davis
      supplemented his income by sending 240 people to their
      deaths from 1890 to 1914, serving the states of New
      York, New Jersey, and Massachusetts, traveling from
      prison to prison in his trademark black felt hat. He was
      the designer of the original electric chair, helped make
      many refinements to the system during his career, and
      held patents on some of the equipment. Before every
      execution he tested the apparatus on chunks of beef,
      attaching sponge pads to the meat, inserting the wires,
      and switching on the current—as soon as the beef began
      to cook, he knew the chair was in full working order.

T*e*n Capital Oddities

1   America executed its last witch in 1692. Poland was still executing witches over a hundred years later, in 1793.

2   The rules for extracting confessions during the Holy Inquisition were spelled out in *The Book of Death*, which was on display in the Casa Santa in Rome until the nineteenth century. There is no record of a single Holy Inquisition acquittal. The accused were rarely told, nor were they ever allowed to ask, what they had been charged with, and they were not permitted a defense counsel or allowed to call witnesses.

3   The authorized method of execution during the reign of the Roman emperor Tiberius was strangulation. Law forbid the strangling of virgins, but the resourceful Tiberius found a loophole: He ordered that virgins should first be defiled by the executioner.

4   In 2005, a neurologist, Dr. Harold Hillman, published his research into the pain caused by various methods of capital punishment. Dr. Hillman described the executioner's technique and the effects upon the victim, tabulating the symptoms of pain showed by them. He concluded that death by stoning is the slowest and therefore probably the most painful way to die.

5   In the Indian state of Baroda in the nineteenth century, the maharajah executed criminals by having elephants step on their heads.

6   On October 9, 1789, during a meeting of the French Legislative Assembly, Joseph Ignace Guillotin, a former

professor of anatomy in the medical faculty of Paris University, proposed that the death penalty should be the same for all social classes and that in all cases some sort of beheading machine should be used. Dr. Guillotin made no further contribution to the development that bore his name. The guillotine in its finished form was the invention of Dr. Antoine Louis, the secretary of the academy of surgery in France. Initially the device was to be called the "louison" or the "louisette" after Dr. Louis, but the name never quite stuck. Nor was the guillotine entirely original; a large wooden structure known as the Halifax Gibbet had been removing heads in England, most Saturday afternoons, since the thirteenth century. It was only one of a hundred similar devices.

7   Two men have survived three hangings apiece. The murderer Joseph Samuels was reprieved in 1803 after the rope broke twice on the first and second attempts and the trapdoor failed to open on the third. A trapdoor mechanism also saved the life of convicted murderer John Lee in 1884. Even though it worked every time it was tested, it failed to open three times in the space of seven minutes. Lee was let off with life imprisonment.

8   Germany retained decapitation by ax as a method of state execution until 1938. Two of the last famous executions by ax were those of Baroness Benita von Falkenhayn and Renate von Natzner, who were accused of spying and lost their heads at the Berlin Plötzensee Prison on February 18, 1935.

9   The electric chair was first used as the "modern" and "humane" alternative to hanging after a forty-year-old murderess, Roxalana Druse, took fifteen minutes to strangle to death in 1887. Three years later, William Kemmler, convicted of the murder of his lover Tillie Ziegler, became the first man to die by the new method. After eight minutes, Kemmler started smoking and a second burst of power was required to finish him off. The *New York Times* reported, "Kemmler was literally roasted to death." The electric chair is still unpredictable. During the execution of Pedro Medina in Florida's "Old Sparky" on March 27, 1997, witnesses saw a foot-long blue-and-orange flame shoot from Medina's head.

10   Thomas Edison, inventor of the lightbulb and the phonograph, pioneered his own version of the electric chair. In 1890, desperate to convince people that the alternating current advocated by his rival George Westinghouse was "unsafe," Edison toured America using AC power to electrocute cats, dogs, horses, and elephants, a process Edison called "Westinghousing."

Ten Most Dubious Legal Defenses in a Criminal Law Court

1   In 1993, Diana Smith, thirty-seven, from Kinsey, Alabama, was found guilty of tampering with a man's grave. The court heard that in 1990, Smith had been charged with causing the death of the man whose grave she had interfered with. She said she was only digging up the casket in order to prove that he was faking it.

2   In 2004, Thubten Dargyel, a fifty-three-year-old Tibetan health-care worker employed in a Wisconsin medical center, was charged with first-degree sexual assault on a woman. He explained that his semen could be found on her clothing because he ejaculated every time he sneezed. Dargyel said that he was surprised that his semen hadn't shown up on many other patients.

3   In 1964, Mexican sisters Delfina and Maria de Jesús González were arrested when police found the remains of at least eighty bodies on the premises of their brothel in Guanajuato. The deadly sisters recruited prostitutes through help-wanted ads and killed them when they outlived their usefulness. When asked for an explanation for the deaths, one of the sisters volunteered, "The food didn't agree with them."

4   In 1994, a court in Virginia dropped charges of rape and sodomy against a forty-five-year-old schizophrenic after accepting evidence that one of the victim's multiple personalities had consented to have sex with one of the rapist's multiple personalities. The prosecution heard that the two had previously met in group therapy and that many of their "different selves" had fallen in love and even talked of marriage.

5   In 2004, a Canadian, Angel Jones, twenty-seven, was convicted of aggravated assault against his girlfriend when he bit off most of her nose during an argument. Jones admitted the nose was in his mouth but claimed that his girlfriend was on a special weight-loss program that had caused her nose to become brittle so it had just fallen off.

6   Thirty-year-old Frederick Treesh was one of three men detained for terrorizing the Great Lakes area with a series of spree killings during the summer of 1994. Treesh explained later, "Other than the two we killed, the two we wounded, the woman we pistol-whipped, and the lightbulbs we stuck in people's mouths, we didn't really hurt anybody."

7   Seattle death-row inmate and convicted murderer Mitchell Rupe, who weighed 270 pounds, appealed against his sentence because he was literally too fat to hang. According to his lawyers, not only would his hanging constitute "cruel and unusual punishment," Rupe might be decapitated by the pressure of his weight on the rope, risking injury "or worse" to onlookers. The appeal failed, and Rupe swung on July 11, 1994.

8   In 1996 in Providence, Rhode Island, Anthony St. Laurent admitted to taking part in organized crime. Upon receiving a ten-month prison sentence, he informed the court that he was really innocent; he had entered a guilty plea only because an illness that

required forty or fifty enemas a day would have made it difficult for him to sit through a very long trial.

9   In 1996, the U.S. Supreme Court rejected the appeal of a convicted Arizona drug user who claimed that he did not receive a fair trial because there were no fat people on the jury.

10   In 2004, Joshua Baldwin, twenty-four, was found guilty of sixteen incidents of indecent exposure to women in shopping malls in downtown Bay City, Michigan. Baldwin told the judge, "I was only hoping to get lucky, but I went about it the wrong way."

Twelve Original Observations Made by Condemned Men

1   "At least I'll get some high-class education"
—Murderer John W. Deering, facing the firing squad,
after willing his body to the University of Utah

2   "Pretty soon you're going to see a baked Appel."
—George Appel, murderer of puns and a New York policeman, as he
was strapped into the electric chair in 1928

3   "Will that gas bother my asthma?"
—Luis José Monge, awaiting death by gassing for the murders of his
wife and three children, at Colorado State Prison in 1967

4   "Warden, I'd like a little bicarb because I'm afraid I'm
going to get gas in my stomach right now."
—Charles de la Roi, sentenced to death by lethal gas in 1946 in
California for the murder of a fellow prison inmate, bidding for the
George Appel Worst Death Chamber Pun Award of 1946

5   "How about this for a headline for tomorrow's paper?
'French fries!' "
—James French, electrocuted in Oklahoma in 1966 (see above)

6   "Just our luck . . . we haven't even got a decent day for it."
—Frank Negran to his fellow murderer Alex Carrion
as they awaited execution at Sing Sing in 1933

7   "Are you sure this thing is safe?"
—The English poisoner Dr. William Palmer as he was escorted to the
gallows trapdoor in 1855, after killing fourteen people

8   "I'd like to thank my family for loving me and taking
care of me. The rest of the world can kiss my ass."
—Robert Alton Harris, gassed on April 21, 1992

9   "I think I'd rather be fishing."
      —Jimmy Glass, electrocuted June 12, 1987

10   "I'm still awake."
      —Robyn Leroy Parks, after his lethal injection on March 10, 1992

11   "You might make that a double."
      —British murderer Neville Heath, gratefully accepting the offer
      of a last drink before being hanged in 1946

12   "I did not get my Spaghetti-O's, I got spaghetti. I want
      the press to know this."
      —Thomas J. Grasso, unimpressed by room service before
      being executed by lethal injection for his role in the murder
      of an elderly Tulsa woman in March 1995

Ten Questionable
Murder Motives

1800: The sensitive Russian Czar Paul, who is both snub-nosed and bald, has a soldier scourged to death for referring to him as "baldy." The Czar later has the words "snub-nosed" and "bald" banned so that his subjects use them on pain of death.

1968: Frustrated rock musician Charles Manson finds hidden messages in the Beatles' album "The Beatles" (popularly known as "the White Album"), especially the tracks "Helter Skelter," "Piggies," and "Revolution 9," which convince him that the apocalypse is at hand. Irked when producer Terry Melcher fails to turn up to hear his songs, Manson and his "family" decide to pay Melcher a visit. Failing to find him at home, they instead brutally murder actress Sharon Tate and four others.

1977: Self-styled emperor of the Central African Republic Jean-Bédel Bokassa has two hundred schoolchildren beaten to death by his imperial guard. Their crime is failure to comply with school uniform regulations.

1979: Two Brazilians, Waldir de Souza and Maria de Conceicao, confess to the murder of six children in Cantigulo, including a two-year-old boy. They say that the killings were ritual sacrifices to ensure success in their new cement business.

1984: A sixteen-year-old Malaysian boy is beheaded by a Chinese man in Kuala Lumpur as a human sacrifice in an attempt to win the state lottery. The murder was in vain, as no one picked a winning number that week.

1987: A Chinese pig farmer, Chen Bohong, of Liuzhou, is about to slaughter a pig when he is rudely interrupted by a taxman, who presents him with a bill. Irritated by the interruption, Chen kills the taxman, Sun Taichang, instead.

1989: A Liberian general, Gray Allison, is sentenced to death for the murder of a policeman. He explains that he needed the policeman's blood to perform a magic rite to overthrow Liberia's dictator, Samuel Doe.

1993: A thirty-six-year-old man from Peking, Ge Yunbao, admits beating a six-year-old schoolboy to death and then leaving the child's severed head on a bus. Yunbao explains that he was annoyed at being passed over for promotion.

1995: During the world population conference held in Cairo, the Egyptian newspaper *Al-Wajd* reports that a delegate has stabbed his wife to death because she refused to go to bed with him.

1996: Francois Gueneron is shot dead by his wife because she can no longer tolerate his habitual flatulence. According to Mrs. Catherine Gueneron, her husband, a forty-four-year-old French construction site manager, broke wind morning, noon, and night for eight years. He took a pistol bullet in the chest from thirty-five-year-old Catherine after farting in her face in bed. She told Marseilles judge Gilbert St. Jacques, "I just snapped."

Chapter Six

The Joy of Sects

Ten Holy Relics

1   At one point, relics claimed to be Christ's foreskin were
    on display in fourteen churches in Italy. Pope Innocent
    III declined to rule on which was the genuine artifact on
    the grounds that God alone knew which was the true
    Holy Foreskin.

2   The personal evacuations of the grand lama of Tibet
    were considered so holy that his followers wore samples
    of his excrement around their necks. His urine was also
    thought to be a powerful prophylactic against disease,
    and his courtiers mixed it into their food.

3   King Henry VII was presented with St. George's left leg
    as a gift.

4   Sri Lanka has a temple dedicated to one of the Buddha's
    teeth.

5   In the nineteenth century, three holy navels of Christ
    were on display in churches at Rome, Lucques, and
    Chalones-sur-Marne.

6   For several decades, the brain of St. Peter was thought to
    be housed above an altar in Geneva, until it turned out to
    be a pumice stone.

7   St. Peter's nail clippings have surfaced in a dozen
    churches in Europe.

8   The body of the Welsh saint Teilo was at one time
    miraculously housed in three different locations.

9   At least sixty churches claim to be the repository of the
    Virgin Mary's breast milk.

10   King Philip II of Spain owned more than 7,000 holy
      relics, including various fragments of the true cross, the
      crown of thorns, 144 heads, 306 arms and legs, and 10
      whole bodies. His personal favorites were the arm of St.
      Vincent and the knee of St. Sebastian.

Ten Causes of the Black Death According to the Church

1   Jews poisoning the wells

2   Going to the theater

3   Olive oil

4   Lust for older women

5   The use of dice

6   Talk of sex

7   Hanging out with witches

8   Overeating

9   Wearing pointed-toed "wincklepicker" shoes

10 The planets Mars and Saturn moving closer together and "turning the air bad"

T*en* Appalling Pontiffs

1   POPE DAMASCUS I (366–384) Left no detail to chance in his campaign to win election as pope by hiring a gang of hit-men to murder the nearest rival for the job and all of his supporters. Nicknamed "the matron's ear-tickler," he enjoyed a reputation as a ladies' man but also surrounded himself with an entourage of sexually ambiguous young men. He was tried, convicted, and sentenced to death for adultery by a synod of forty-four bishops in 378 A.D. but was pardoned by the emperor.

2   POPE STEPHEN VI (896–897) Not on the best of terms with his predecessor, Pope Formosus, Pope Stephen had the corpse of the ex-pope dug up and tried by the "Cadaver Synod" for crimes against the Church. A few months later he was overthrown, imprisoned, and strangled to death in his cell.

3   POPE JOHN XII "THE BAD" (955–963) He held orgies at his home and, during one of the raunchier sessions, was accused of summoning the devil. He and his friends also liked to molest female pilgrims inside the basilica of St. Peter: When a cardinal pointed out that this wasn't theologically sound practice, the pope had him castrated. Found guilty in absentia of various crimes including incest, adultery, and murder, Pope John was excommunicated and later bludgeoned to death with a hammer by an irate husband who found him in bed with his wife.

4   POPE JOHN XXI (1276–77) The only doctor ever to become pope, he was originally appointed physician to

178

the Vatican on the strength of a medical treatise in which he prescribed lettuce leaves for toothache, lettuce seed to reduce sex drive, and pig dung to stop nosebleeds. While receiving his medical advice, three popes— Gregory X (1271–76), Innocent V (1276), and Adrian V (1276)—died in quick succession. He was duly elected pontiff, possibly in the hope that his medical skills would enable him to live longer than the previous three. Twelve months after his election, the roof of his new palace fell in, crushing him horribly, and he died six days later.

5   POPE BONIFACE VIII (1294–1305) Boniface got rid of his predecessor, Pope Celestine V, by locking him up in Fumone castle and leaving him to die of starvation. Boniface was an atheist who had numerous gay lovers and was eventually tried for heresy, rape, sodomy, and eating meat during Lent. Boniface didn't attend his trial and escaped punishment, but went mad soon afterward and committed suicide. Pope Clement V had Boniface's body exhumed and burned as a heretic.

6   POPE LEO X (1313–21) The patron of Michelangelo and Raphael, Leo was promiscuously gay; when he was elected he was suffering so much from anal ulcerations that he had to be carried into the conclave on a stretcher. It was Pope Leo who provoked Martin Luther to nail his ninety-six theses to the door of the church in Wittenberg to denounce Church corruption.

7   POPE JOHN XXIII (1410–15) A former pirate who obtained the papacy through force of arms, he was

charged in 1415 with fifty-four offenses, including piracy, murder, rape, sodomy, and incest. There were originally seventy charges, but sixteen said to be "of the most indescribable depravity" were dropped in the interest of public decency.

8 POPE SIXTUS IV (1471–84) Builder of the Sistine Chapel. His less artistic achievements included six illegitimate sons, one of them the result of an incestuous relationship with his sister, and a papal bull unleashing the Spanish Inquisition and the subsequent torture and burning of thousands of heretics.

9 POPE ALEXANDER VI (1492–1503) The only pontiff to travel in public with a retinue of scantily clad dancing girls and the first to introduce the concept of entertainments featuring naked women at Mass, Alexander secured the papal chair by bribery and then used it for the personal gain of his growing family, the infamous Borgias. His ten illegitimate children included a favorite daughter, Lucretia. At one point the pope was enjoying incestuous relations with Lucretia while she in turn was sleeping with her own brother, Cesare. Alexander also threw the Vatican's most outrageous party, the "Joust of Whores," featuring a variety of entertainments including a prize for the guest who slept with the most prostitutes. While the pope and his teenage mistress and various civic dignitaries looked on, fifty naked prostitutes recruited from the city slums slithered around on the marble floor picking up chestnuts with their labia.

10   POPE PAUL III (1534–49) Rome's biggest pimp, Paul
kept some 45,000 prostitutes who paid him a monthly
tribute. He also poisoned several relatives, including his
mother and his niece, to gain control of his family
inheritance, and he enjoyed an incestuous relationship
with his daughter. He once killed a couple of cardinals
and a Polish bishop to settle an argument over a
theological point.

Beyond Belief:
Ten Routes to Sainthood

1 St. Denis is the patron saint of syphilis and of Paris. He was beheaded, but he carried his head around with him. He is not to be confused with St. Fiacre, the patron saint of nonspecific venereal disease, a job he combines with looking after gardeners and hemorrhoid sufferers (after an altercation with a nonbeliever in Brittany, St. Fiacre sat down heavily on a rock, miraculously leaving the impression of his buttocks upon it. Christian hemorrhoid and acne sufferers later claimed that they could get relief by sitting where St. Fiacre had rested).

2 St. Agatha is the patron saint of Malta, bell-makers, diseases of the breast, earthquakes, fire, and sterility. In the third century, she defended her virginity against a high-ranking Roman and was sent to prison, where her breasts were cut off; they were restored by divine intervention. She was sent to work in a brothel (where her virginity miraculously remained intact), then burned at the stake, where she failed to ignite. Finally she was beheaded. Sicilians honor her feast day every year by carrying an image of her breasts through the streets.

3 The feast day of St. Lawrence is August 10. He was roasted alive on a spit, but faced death heroically, telling his torturers, "Turn me over—I'm cooked on that side." St. Lawrence is the patron saint of those who grill.

4 September 18 is the feast day of the seventeenth-century "flying monk," St. Joseph of Copertino. During Mass he was seen to hover about twelve paces above the ground while "uttering his customary shrill cry." Pope Urban

VIII once saw him in flight and was full of admiration, but his feats of levitation didn't go down well with everyone, especially his fellow monks, who regarded his flying as a nuisance.

5   December 19 is the feast day of the Blessed William of Fenoli, a monk who lived in the thirteenth century. One day, while accompanied by his mule, he was attacked by robbers. William defended himself by ripping off the leg of his mule and clubbing his attackers with it. Then he restored the leg and continued on his journey.

6   The feast day of the sibling saints Eulampius and Eulampia, brother and sister martyrs, is celebrated on November 10. In fourth-century Turkey, during the reign of Gallienius, the couple survived being boiled in oil, which moved 200 astonished onlookers to convert to Christianity on the spot. By the order of the emperor, all 200 converts were beheaded.

7   St. Nicholas is the patron saint of Russia, children, pawnbrokers, unmarried girls, perfumers, and sailors. He was a bishop in southwestern Turkey during the fourth century and is purported to have restored to full health three decapitated children. St. Nicholas was said to have been such a pious baby that he abstained from his mother's milk on Wednesdays and Fridays.

8   The feast day of St. Swithun is July 2. Known as "the drunken saint" (*The Oxford Companion to the Year* notes that this is "probably a jocular reference to heavy

rainfall"), St. Swithun performed only one recorded miracle, and a relatively modest one at that. A woman on her way to market dropped her basket of eggs, breaking all of them. Swithun said a prayer for her and when the woman looked into the basket again the eggs had unscrambled themselves and returned to salable condition. To test his awesome powers of self-control, Swithun liked to sleep chastely between two beautiful virgins.

9   The feast day of St. Simeon the Stylite is January 5. The most famous of the "pillar hermits," he was known for his thrift and for living on top of a column for thirty years. He demonstrated his divinity by standing on one leg for a year and tying a rope around his waist so tightly that his lower body became putrefied and infested with maggots. He simply ate the maggots, saying, "Eat what God has given you." He passed out, but was revived with a few lettuce leaves. St. Simeon bowed in prayer one day and fell off his pole to his death.

10   The feast day of St. Catherine of Siena is April 29. She overcame her fear of bubonic plague victims by drinking a whole bowl of pus.

Ten Things You Are Very Unlikely to Learn in Sunday School

1   The Book of Esther is the only book in the Bible that neglects to mention God.

2   Although the Church has always frowned on adultery, it didn't get around to banning sex with animals until the Council of Ankara in A.D. 314.

3   The modern confessional box was invented in the Middle Ages to help stop priests from sexually assaulting women.

4   The early Christian Church held that the Virgin Mary was impregnated by her ear: Fear of accidental aural penetration was so widespread that it led to the fashion for tight-fitting wimples.

5   The Catholic Church accepts cannibalism as a justifiable means of saving one's life.

6   Onan, the son of Judah, who "spilled his seed" in the Old Testament (Genesis 38:9) is the Bible's only masturbator. The passage was the basis for the Church's condemnation of the practice and gave rise to the word "onanism," in Victorian times a popular term for self-abuse.

7   The Old Testament Book of Ecclesiastes recommends clearing the stomach by throwing up before or during a big meal to make room for more food.

8   The Bible is full of lepers because it was written at a time when any skin defect, even a bad case of acne, was likely to get you branded as a leper and consequently shunned by society. Most "lepers" probably suffered from syphilis.

9   The Church adopted celibacy as a code for the priesthood in 1123. Three hundred and fifty years later, Pope Innocent VIII became known as "the Honest" because he admitted that he had fathered several bastards. He owned up only to disprove a rumor going around Rome at the time that he was a woman.

10   Before the Reformation, men could be excommunicated for wearing wigs. The Church required men's hair to be short, straight, and "unadorned."

Chapter Seven

Unstrung Heroes

Ten Lesser-Known Scientific Endeavors

1   Sir Isaac Newton spent thirty of the most productive
    years of his life trying to change base metals into gold
    and searching for hidden codes in the Bible, which he
    believed contained God's secret laws for the universe. He
    said that the mathematical formulae in his *Philosophiae
    Naturalis Principia Mathematica*, which contains some of
    the cornerstones of modern science, were first revealed
    by God to a group of mystics at the dawn of civilization,
    a tradition to which he had been chosen as heir, and he
    predicted that the world would end in 2060. The man
    who possessed perhaps the greatest scientific mind of all
    also cut two cat-flaps in his front door, one for his cat and
    a smaller one for the cat's kitten.

2   Charles Babbage, the "father of computing," devoted
    much of his spare time to working out the statistical
    probability of the biblical miracles. He calculated that
    the chances of a man rising from the dead were 1 in
    1,012. Babbage was also obsessed with fire and water. He
    once allowed himself to be baked in an oven at 265° F
    for "five or six minutes without any great discomfort,"
    and he almost drowned while testing a device for
    walking on water.

3   Charles Waterton, the eighteenth-century British
    adventurer-naturalist, became famous after the
    publication in 1826 of his book *Wandering in South
    America*, the result of many years spent alone in
    unexplored rain forest. The book combined accurate
    observations of wildlife, including the very first account
    of sloths, with idiosyncratic notes on politics and

taxidermy and a vicious attack on the Hanoverian
monarchy. Waterton took a hands-on approach to his
fieldwork, once spending six months sleeping with his
foot dangling out of his hammock in the hope that he
would be bitten by a vampire bat. He was "bitterly
disappointed" when "the brutes failed to take the bait."

4   Charles Darwin, having calculated the precise number of
earthworms in his garden (an average of 53,767 per
acre), piled thousands of them on his billiard table and
subjected them to a series of experiments, including
studies of what happened when he blew tobacco smoke
at them and when his son played a bassoon at them.
After placing some worms close to the keys of a piano,
which was played as loudly as possible, Darwin deduced:
"Worms do not possess any sense of hearing." He later
repeated the experiment by playing a bassoon to his
plants and again deduced that his subjects were deaf.

5   Sir Francis Galton, a cousin of Charles Darwin, was said
to have had an IQ of 200, the highest ever recorded. He
invented fingerprinting, was a pioneer in the science of
eugenics, and was the first to describe high- and low-
pressure weather patterns. He also invented a pocket
counting device used to clock the number of attractive
women he passed in the street to help him compile a
"beauty map" of Great Britain: After many years of
dedicated research, Galton determined that Britain's
ugliest women lived in Aberdeen. His finest hour came in
1850, when he became the first European to explore
Damaraland in Southwest Africa. Upon encountering the

Hottentot people, he turned his analytical mind to the measurement of African ladies' bottoms.

6   Alexander Graham Bell, who kept his windows permanently covered to keep out the "harmful rays" of the full moon, tried to teach his dog to talk and dissected the family cat in order to study its vocal cords. Bell also experimented with livestock: Convinced that sheep with extra nipples would give birth to more lambs, he spent thirty years counting sheep nipples. He abandoned his research when the U.S. State Department officially announced it could find no link between multiple nipples and increased fertility.

7   The English scientist J. B. S. Haldane, a pioneer in genetics, subjected himself to various experiments. He once drank a bottle of hydrochloric acid and then bicycled home to see what effect it would have; he then swallowed a near-fatal dose of calcium chloride, which resulted in violent diarrhea followed by painful constipation. To test his lung capacity, he swallowed one and a half ounces of bicarbonate of soda, then ran up and down a 150-foot flight of stairs twenty times, causing himself to have a fit, during which he crushed several of his vertebrae. Haldane was also prepared to experiment on others without necessarily asking for permission. While lecturing at a public meeting on the dangers of gas in trench warfare, he vaporized a spoonful of pepper over an oil lamp, causing the hall to fill with pungent smoke. As people fled for the exits, eyes streaming and lungs gasping for air, he shouted after them, "If that

upsets you, how would you like a deluge of poison gas from an air fleet in real war?"

8   The pioneer of the miner's lamp, Sir Humphrey Davy, was an avid angler and thought he could baffle his quarry if he disguised himself as a form of natural greenery by wearing a green coat, green trousers, and a green hat. According to a fellow angler, "Davy flattered himself he resembled vegetable life as closely as it was possible to do." When Davy went shooting, however, he did exactly the opposite. Not very trusting of the marksmanship of his fellow sportsmen, he made himself as conspicuous as possible to avoid being accidentally shot by wearing bright-colored clothing and a huge, wide-brimmed, bright red hat.

9   Nikola Tesla, whose name ranks with those of Thomas Edison and Guglielmo Marconi as one of the greats in the history of electricity, studied birds in the local woods and then jumped from the roof of the family barn, clutching an umbrella, convinced he could fly. This line of research was abandoned after he spent six weeks in traction.

10   The aviator Orville Wright numbered the eggs that his chickens produced so he could eat them in the precise order in which they had been laid. He also had a morbid fear of public appearances. When President Franklin Roosevelt went to Wright's hometown, Dayton Ohio, to campaign for reelection, Orville reluctantly agreed to

have lunch with him. Later, however, when he found himself in the back of the president's touring car being driven though cheering crowds, at the first opportunity he jumped out, thanked the president for lunch, and then walked home.

Shot in the Foot:
Ten Military Bloopers

532 B.C.: Croesus, king of Lydia, asks the Delphic oracle if he should attack the Persians. She replies, "Cross the river Halys and attack and you will destroy a great nation." He does, and destroys his own.

1199: King Richard I, "the Lionheart," pauses to admire an arrow fired directly at him at Chalus. It hits him in the shoulder. As he lies dying of blood poisoning, he congratulates the bowman on his skill.

1632: Gustavus Adolphus, king of Sweden, refuses to wear any steel body armor at the Battle of Lützen, saying, "The Lord God is my armor!" He is killed.

1836: Mexican general Antonio Lopez de Santa Anna and his troops find themselves near a wood known to be full of Texan soldiers, but they insist on taking their usual afternoon siesta. While Santa Anna and his men quietly snooze, the Texans attack and rout the entire Mexican army in less than twenty minutes.

1849: At Chillianwalla, nearsighted Brigadier Pope faces his cavalry in the wrong direction and leads them in a charge away from the battlefield.

1862: General "Stonewall" Jackson, a strict Presbyterian who refuses to fight on Sundays, spends the day praying alone during the thick of the battle of Mechanicsville, refusing to speak to anyone while his troops take heavy casualties.

1864: Major General John Sedgwick, unimpressed by Confederate sniper fire at the battle of Spotsylvania, scoffs: "What! What! Men dodging this way from a single bullet! I am ashamed of you. They couldn't hit an elephant at this dist . . ."

1869:   Francisco Lopez, the president of Paraguay, wages a hopeless war on three fronts against his neighboring enemies Argentina, Brazil, and Uruguay. He is outnumbered ten to one by their combined armies. Lopez decides to make up the numbers by sending out a battalion of twelve-year-olds wearing false beards.

1879:   British Lord Chelmsford invades Zululand but suspects that the Zulus might not fight. At Isandlwana, 1,300 British troops are slaughtered. Fifty-five survive.

1944:   Erwin Rommel, Hitler's commander entrusted with the defense of France's Channel coast against a possible Allied invasion, decides on the eve of D-Day that it is so quiet he might as well go home and celebrate his wife's birthday.

T𝑒𝑛 Former Occupations of Dictators

1   JOSEPH STALIN, RULER OF THE SOVIET UNION,
    1929–53 Trainee priest

2   JOSIP BROZ (MARSHAL TITO), PRESIDENT OF
    YUGOSLAVIA, 1945–80 Locksmith

3   RAFAEL TRUJILLO, PRESIDENT OF THE
    DOMINICAN REPUBLIC, 1930–61, and
    GENERAL NE WIN, PRESIDENT OF BURMA,
    1962–88 Post office clerks

4   BENITO MUSSOLINI, RULER OF ITALY,
    1922–43, and MAO ZEDONG, CHAIRMAN OF
    THE PEOPLE'S REPUBLIC OF CHINA,
    1931–76 Trainee teachers

5   "PAPA DOC" DUVALIER, RULER OF HAITI,
    1957–71 Family doctor

6   ENVER HOXHA, RULER OF ALBANIA,
    1945–85 Tobacconist

7   FERDINAND MARCOS, PRESIDENT OF THE
    PHILIPPINES, 1965–86 Criminal lawyer

8   NICOLAE CEAUŞESCU, PRESIDENT OF
    ROMANIA, 1965–89 Shoemaker

9   POL POT, RULER OF CAMBODIA, 1975–79 Buddhist
    monk

10 IDI AMIN, PRESIDENT OF UGANDA, 1971–79
    Doughnut vendor

Ten Household Accessories Belonging to Serial Killer Ed Gein

1   Lamp shades made from human skin

2   A belt made from nipples

3   Four noses and a heart

4   A table with shinbone legs

5   A bowl made from the top of a human skull

6   Salted female genitals in a shoe box

7   A pair of lips on a string curtain pull

8   A shirt of human skin complete with female breasts

9   The faces of nine women, mounted on a wall

10   A head with large nails hammered through each ear

T*en* Kleptocrats

1 JOSEPH MOBUTU, PRESIDENT OF ZAIRE
So rich, it was said, he could write a personal check to
pay off his country's entire foreign debt. Although his
country was one of the world's poorest, he chartered
a French Concorde jet to fly his family to Europe on
monthly shopping trips, and had pink champagne flown
in from Paris and prostitutes delivered from Scandinavia.
He sent a government jet to Venezuela thirty-two times
to ferry back five thousand longhaired sheep so he could
build himself a model farm in the Zaire jungle.

2 JEAN-BÉDEL BOKASSA, RULER OF THE
CENTRAL AFRICAN REPUBLIC His country was
officially rated the poorest in Africa, but he spent $18
million on a forty-eight-hour coronation binge to
celebrate his "promotion" from president to emperor in
1977. At the coronation ceremony, which required the
purchase of 100 limousines and 130 thoroughbred horses,
guests drank about 65,000 bottles of champagne served
by an army of waiters imported from Paris and were
entertained by a 120-piece orchestra.

3 FERDINAND MARCOS, PRESIDENT OF THE
PHILIPPINES He appropriated up to one-third of all
loans to the Philippines in the form of kickbacks and
commissions and oversaw foreign investment in his
country for a "small fee"; a U.S. nuclear power company
once paid him tens of millions of dollars in bribes to
allow them to build on Philippines land. As it turned out,
it was money not well spent: The power station was
never used, having been built over an earthquake zone.

At one time, Marcos's wife Imelda, apart from her influence as a world-class buyer of fashion footwear, was said to be the world's single biggest buyer of jewelry.

4   NICOLAE CEAUŞESCU, PRESIDENT OF ROMANIA He bulldozed the center of Bucharest to make way for a monumental avenue leading to the world's largest palace, an architectural eyesore incorporating the work of about seven hundred interior designers, second in size only to the Pentagon and featuring a marble-lined nuclear bunker. The construction of the new Palace of the People required the destruction of dozens of historic buildings, including twenty-six churches, and it forced about forty thousand people to give up their homes in exchange for small apartments in a grim concrete residential block. Romanian TV newswomen were forbidden to wear jewelry so they would not appear more glamorous than their first lady, Elena Ceauşescu.

5   FRANÇOIS "PAPA DOC" DUVALIER, PRESIDENT OF HAITI He raised corruption to an art form, diverting millions of dollars in foreign-aid money into his own bank account. "Papa Doc" also hit upon a way of literally bleeding his own people dry by rounding up thousands of Haitians and marching them to the nearest blood bank, where each was given $1.80—about a week's wages—in exchange for a quart of blood. The blood was then sold to the United States, where it was resold for transfusion at $22 a quart. "Papa Doc" dreamed of building a permanent memorial to his

megalomania, a new Haitian city called Duvalierville.
Haitian telephone subscribers were surprised to find that
they had been charged an extra levy to fund the building
project, especially as their country's telephone system had
not worked for twenty years.

6   JEAN-CLAUDE "BABY DOC" DUVALIER,
PRESIDENT OF HAITI When his father, "Papa Doc,"
died, he became at nineteen the youngest president in
the world. In 1981, the International Monetary Fund
gave $22 million to the treasury of Haiti, only to discover
two days later that $20 million of it had been withdrawn
by "Baby Doc." Much of the money funded the
extravagant lifestyle of his wife Michele, including
$50,000 a month to fly flowers from Miami to Haiti. She
always turned the air conditioning up to maximum so
she could wear her fur coats indoors.

7   KING ZOG OF ALBANIA In 1939, an invasion by
Mussolini forced Albania's despot and his wife to flee
into exile, accompanied by the entire national treasury.
The Zogs sat out the war years in the Ritz in London,
where they thought it wise to sell their bright-red
Mercedes, a wedding present from Adolf Hitler that was
inconveniently identical to the one used by the Führer
himself.

8   KIM JONG-IL, PRESIDENT OF NORTH KOREA
He is the world's biggest single buyer of French cognac:
The Dear Leader's annual spending on his favorite tipple,
which costs $1,300 a bottle in Seoul, is nearly eight

hundred times the income of the average North Korean citizen. Kim Jong-Il also maintains a harem of about two thousand imported blondes and young Asian women, his "Joy Brigade" comprising a "satisfaction team" for sexual favors, a "happiness team" for massages, and a "dancing team" for postcoital karaoke and dancing performances.

9   JOAQUÍN BALAGUER, PRESIDENT OF THE DOMINICAN REPUBLIC Balaguer bankrupted his country by spending millions on a massive illuminated cross, intended to commemorate the 500th anniversary of the arrival of Christopher Columbus in the Americas. Slums were razed to make way for the project and escalating costs led to soaring food prices. Balaguer was forced to cancel the opening ceremony in 1990 when he was snubbed by his invited guests, the king of Spain and the pope. When the illumination was finally switched on for the first time, it caused a disastrous drain on the national grid—unnoticed, however, by the 60 percent of the country's people who still did not have electricity.

10   SANI ABACHA, MILITARY DICTATOR OF NIGERIA He stole more than $4 billion during his five-year reign. Abacha died of a heart attack in 1998, aged fifty-four, during a Viagra-fueled romp with three Indian prostitutes. A few weeks after his death, police at Kano airport became suspicious when his widow, Maryam, tried to leave the country with thirty-eight pieces of luggage. Each was found to be stuffed with U.S. dollars. Mrs. Abacha explained that she was not stealing the money, just "putting away the funds in some foreign

accounts for safekeeping." To dispel any lingering suspicions that she may have had anything to hide, she hired the services of O. J. Simpson's legal expert Johnnie Cochran. The Nigerian government agreed to drop charges in exchange for the return of the billions of dollars sent to foreign bank accounts while her husband was in office.

Ten Monarchs Madder than King George III

1 **KING CHARLES VI "THE FOOLISH" OF FRANCE (C. 1380–1422)** Early in his reign, he was struck down by a mystery illness that made his hair and nails fall out. He made a complete physical recovery but lived on in equally complete mental derangement, often given to bouts of extreme violence for most of his thirty-year rule. His physicians tried to cure him with shock treatment by arranging for seventeen men with blackened faces to hide in his room; when Charles entered, they all jumped out and shouted "Boo!" In one of his more lucid moments, he found out that his wife had taken a lover, the Count of Armagnac: Charles had him strangled and drowned in the River Seine.

2 **SULTAN MURAD IV OF TURKEY (C. 1623–40)** Murad set himself a goal of taking ten lives a day, beheading anyone who annoyed him. He also enjoyed daily target-practice with his long-barreled gun, shooting at innocent passersby who strayed too close to his bedroom window. Murad once came across a party of women who were enjoying a picnic and had them all drowned because they were making too much noise. He killed one of his doctors by forcing to him to swallow an overdose of opium and murdered a musician for humming a Persian tune. Wherever he traveled, his stopping-off points were usually marked by spot executions of smokers—another of his pet hates. In the first five years of his reign he had about 25,000 people put to death, and he killed many of them himself.

3   KING CHRISTIAN VII OF DENMARK
(C. 1766–1808) This king indulged in violent wrecking
sprees around his palace, often beating his head against
walls until he drew blood. He spent his evenings stalking
the streets of Copenhagen with a gang of friends,
occasionally destroying brothels. He lived the last twenty
years of his life in seclusion and was completely crazy,
though he was dragged out to make an occasional
ceremonial appearance. Little was known of the king's
mental condition outside royal circles; even when the full
story broke years later, Danish history books taught that
Christian had simply become a little odd because he had
been sexually abused by pageboys when he was a child.

4   KING FREDERICK WILLIAM I OF PRUSSIA
(C. 1713–40) A close relative of King George III, the
"Soldier King" carried a rattan stick, which he used to
thrash anyone in sight, including members of his own
household. At mealtimes he threw plates and silverware,
attacked his servants, and either starved his children or
spat in their food. He kept two pistols loaded with salt by
his side: One valet had his eye shot out, another was
crippled. His courtiers were so afraid of him that when
one of them was summoned to the king's private
quarters he dropped dead with fright. On his deathbed,
the king was visited by a priest who read from the Book
of Job: "Naked came I out of my mother's womb and
naked shall I return thither." "Not quite naked," the king
corrected him. "I shall have my uniform on."

5 KING FERDINAND VI OF SPAIN (C. 1746–59)
The only son of the mentally disturbed King Philip V,
his reign was marked by a series of increasingly
desperate suicide attempts during which he alternately
tried starving and eating himself to death, cut his wrists
with scissors, hanged himself with bedsheets, and
strangled himself with table napkins. When all else
failed, he begged his doctors to give him poison. He died
of natural causes in his sleep at age forty-six.

6 QUEEN MARIA I "THE MAD" OF PORTUGAL
(C. 1777–1816) In 1788, a smallpox epidemic carried
away several members of Maria's immediate family,
including her son José. According to legend, the
combined shock of these deaths made her violently
unstable; she also took to wearing children's clothes.

7 EMPEROR FERDINAND I OF AUSTRIA
(C. 1835–48) Born hydrocephalic (with water on the
brain), he grew up to be a violent epileptic who could
barely sign his own name and was otherwise incapable.
His tongue was too big for his mouth—an inherited
Habsburg defect—and he found it difficult to string a
sentence together. His idea of a good time was to wedge
his backside into a wastebasket and roll around the floor
in it. In 1848, he was persuaded to abdicate in favor of
his eighteen-year-old nephew Franz Joseph and was
spirited away from Vienna to a mental institution at
Olmutz in Moravia, where he died in his eighty-third
year.

8   KING LUDWIG II OF BAVARIA (C. 1863–86) The
     most famous son of the House of Wittelsbach, a German
     royal family with a long tradition of mental instability,
     Ludwig had two obsessions: an expensive patronage of
     the composer Richard Wagner and an even more
     expensive hobby of erecting fantastic mock-medieval
     castles, which he called his "sick children." Ludwig tried
     to fund his building program by sending begging letters
     to the crowned heads of Europe, then by planning a
     series of major bank robberies; neither attempt was
     successful, so in 1873 he tried to "sell" Bavaria. With the
     treasury in a state of near bankruptcy, the government
     pronounced the king incurably insane and placed him
     under house arrest. Ludwig eluded permanent
     internment by drowning himself in Lake Stern.

9   SULTAN MURAD V (C. 1876) His reign was the
     briefest of all the Ottoman sultans. Just three months
     after his accession, Murad, who was alcoholic, obviously
     unbalanced, and incapable of performing any sort of
     official function, was quietly locked away after an
     Austrian doctor and a Turkish court physician jointly
     signed a document declaring that he was incurably
     insane.

10   KING OTTO I OF BAVARIA (1848–1916) He
     became king when his elder brother Ludwig II (see
     above) was pronounced insane and removed from the
     throne. Ironically, Otto was even crazier than the king he
     replaced, but whereas his older brother had earned
     notoriety by organizing pan-European bank robberies

and the undying gratitude of the German tourist industry by building fantastic castles, Otto's mental illness manifested itself in the less-notable activities of barking like a dog, shouting abuse, and occasionally taking potshots at people through his bedroom window with a rifle. Otto reigned in name only from his cell in Castle Fürstenried, guarded by a few medical attendants for twenty-seven years while his uncle Luitpold took charge of Bavaria as prince-regent.

Uneasy Lies the Head:
Ten Paranoid Rulers

1   EMPEROR QIN SHI HUANGDI (C. 246–210 B.C.)
China's first emperor maintained his rule with a
combination of enthusiastic wall-building to keep out his
external enemies and removal of the tongues, hands,
feet, and genitalia of his enemies within. To ensure that
no unfavorable comparisons were made between his own
and earlier regimes, he ordered the mass burning of all
of China's history books and decapitated the region's top
160 academics. The emperor took his paranoia with him
to his grave; his giant mausoleum was guarded by eight
thousand life-sized terra cotta soldiers to ward off the
ghosts of the thousands of people he had wronged in his
lifetime.

2   CZAR PAUL I (1796–1801) Morbidly suspicious of
democracy and of anything Western European, Paul
banned the import of books and censored correspondence
with foreigners. He closed down private printing presses
and deleted from the Russian dictionary the words
"citizen," "club," "society," and "revolution." In 1797, he
made a law banning modern dress including round hats,
top boots, long pants, and shoes with laces, then sent a
couple of hundred armed troops onto the streets of St.
Petersburg with orders to attack anyone who didn't
conform to his dress code. He was strangled in a palace
coup.

3   KING HENRI CHRISTOPHE OF HAITI (1811–18)
He insisted on drawing attention to his country's chief
export by having himself anointed with chocolate syrup.

He became obsessed with his personal security and ordered all his bodyguards to prove their loyalty by marching over the edge of a two-hundred-foot cliff to certain death: Those who disobeyed were tortured and executed.

4   JOSÉ GASPAR RODRÍGUEZ DE FRANCIA Y VELASCO (C. 1818–40) The first of a long line of Paraguayan dictators was constantly haunted by the fear of assassination and created a vast network of spies. Whenever he went out, no one else was allowed on the streets, and doors and windows of houses had to be shuttered: Anyone caught on the street when he passed had to prostrate himself or risk being put to the sword by his escort of armed cavalry. He had every tree and shrub in Ascuncion removed in case they hid assassins. Eventually, Francia, as he preferred to be called, became a total recluse, hiding in his palace and attended by just four servants, employing his sister to unroll his cigars to see if they had been tampered with, and communicating with the outside world only through his barber.

5   SULTAN ABDUL HAMID II (C. 1876–1909) Although protected by a steel-lined fez and a personal bodyguard of several thousand tall Albanians, Abdul "the Damned" considered security at his palaces far too lax and set about building a new, impregnable palace from scratch, with every wall mirrored so that he could see the people around him from any angle, every door lined with steel, and all the rooms connected by secret underground

passages that only Abdul Hamid knew about. The sultan always carried a pearl-handled revolver with him. A nervous, jumpy little man, he was a crack shot—a lethal combination. When one of his gardeners made too sudden a bowing movement, Abdul Hamid shot him in the head. The sultan's greatest phobia was fear of poisoning—his was the only dairy herd in the world with a twenty-four-hour bodyguard. Whenever news reached him of assassination attempts elsewhere in Europe, he banned all mention of them in the press: When the king and queen of Serbia were butchered and then tossed out of a bedroom window in 1903, the Turkish press solemnly reported that they had both died of indigestion.

6 JOSEPH STALIN (C. 1924–53) Stalin ensured his survival by removing all political rivals—in a single day in December 1938, "Uncle Joe" signed 3,182 death warrants. He once became depressed and called on the famous Russian neurologist and psychiatrist Vladimir Bekhterev. The doctor diagnosed "grave paranoia" and advised Stalin to retire immediately. It was the last advice Bekhterev ever gave; arrangements for his funeral were made soon afterward. Stalin was about to launch his biggest leadership purge yet when he was felled by a terminal stroke.

7 KING ZOG OF ALBANIA (1928–39) Having survived an estimated fifty-five assassination attempts, Zog made a point of never appearing in public except on national holidays; as he was well over six feet tall and had red hair,

he made a conspicuous target in a country where most men were dark and under five feet six. On the very rare occasions when he ventured outside, his mother acted as chaperon, because according to the strict rules of the Albanian blood feud, no man could be harmed if accompanied in public by a woman. His nerves were so frayed that on his wedding day he banned photographers' flashbulbs, and not once during the ten days of commanded public rejoicing did he or his bride, the Hungarian countess Geraldine Apponyi, dare to appear at the palace window to acknowledge their subjects.

8 ENVER HOXHA, PRESIDENT OF ALBANIA (1945–85) He lived in fear of joint invasion by "Anglo-American imperialists" and "Russo-Bulgar revisionists." In 1950, he ordered the construction of a prototype concrete bunker, complete with a sniper's gun slit with 360-degree visibility. When the small, mushroom-shaped edifice was complete, he asked the chief engineer if he was confident that it could withstand a full assault from a tank. The man replied in the affirmative. Hoxha then insisted that the engineer stand inside his creation while it was bombarded by a tank. After fifteen minutes the shell-shocked engineer emerged, shaken and deaf, but unscathed. Hoxha was impressed and immediately ordered mass construction of the bunkers. From 1950 until his death in 1985, he built about 800,000 of them, one for every four Albanians, covering the entire countryside and costing from one-third to one-half of his

nation's pitifully small resources. No one invaded, but the
bunkers remain Hoxha's legacy to this day.

9   PRESIDENT MACIS NGUEMA, RULER OF
EQUATORIAL GUINEA (1968–79) Nguema wiped
out real or imagined enemies, which turned out to be
more than 10 percent of his country's 350,000
population, including ten of his original twelve cabinet
members, averaging about one political killing per week.
He ordered the assassination of the ambassador to the
United Nations, had a priest frozen to death in a
refrigeration truck, and amputated the fingers of his
government statistician because "he couldn't count."

10 NICOLAE CEAUŞESCU, PRESIDENT OF
ROMANIA (1965–89) He operated the world's most
pervasive surveillance system: Every Romanian
telephone manufactured during his dictatorship was
fitted with a bugging device. After receiving an
anonymous death threat through the mail, he ordered his
secret police to secure handwriting samples from the
entire Romanian population. In 1978, Ceauşescu and his
wife Elena stayed at Buckingham Palace; the queen was
baffled when her guests brought with them their own
bed linen (both had a germ phobia) plus a host of
bodyguards, including a personal food-taster. She was also
alarmed by Nicolae's habit of washing his hands
afterward every time he shook hands with anyone, a trick
he repeated after shaking hands with the queen herself.

Leaders at Leisure:
Ten Hobbies of Dictators

1   JOSEPH STALIN, LEADER OF THE SOVIET
UNION, 1941–53 Watching American movies. He saw
his favorite, the 1938 *Boys Town* starring Spencer Tracy,
at least twenty-five times.

2   ADOLF HITLER, CHANCELLOR OF GERMANY,
1933–45 Reading cheap cowboy-Western novels. His
favorite author was Karl May.

3   NICOLAE CEAUȘESCU, PRESIDENT OF
ROMANIA, 1965–89 Bear hunting.

4   IDI AMIN: PRESIDENT OF UGANDA, 1971–79
Watching cartoons. When police searched his home in
1979, they found a large case full of old film reels of
"Tom & Jerry."

5   KIM JONG-IL, LEADER OF NORTH KOREA
FROM 1997 Watching videos. He owns more than
twenty thousand. He is also believed to be Asia's biggest
collector of pornography.

6   JOSEPH MOBUTU, PRESIDENT OF ZAIRE,
1965–97 Shopaholic. His garden had a runway big
enough to land the Air France Concorde that he regularly
took to buy his groceries from Paris and Brussels.

7   SAPARMURAT NIYAZOV, PRESIDENT OF
TURKMENISTAN FROM 1991 Writing poetry. His
literary works include the epic *White Wheat*, dedicated to
Turkmenistan's harvest, and *Mother*, dedicated to his late
mother, with whom he is said to be obsessed.

8   BENITO MUSSOLINI Creative writing. Mussolini
     published more than fourteen volumes in and out of
     office, including a bodice-ripper, *The Cardinal's Mistress*,
     and a critique of the Russian novel. In his final idle
     moments, before he was strung upside down by piano
     wire, Il Duce was translating Giosuè Carducci's *Odi
     Barbare* into German.

9   MUAMMAR GADDAFI, PRESIDENT OF LIBYA
     FROM 1969 Surfing the Internet.

10   SADDAM HUSSEIN, PRESIDENT OF IRAQ,
     1979–2003 Fishing. He had little time for the subtleties
     of angling, preferring to lob hand grenades into the
     water and then have someone pick up the dead fish.

Chapter Eight

Miscellany

Bark at the Moon:
Ten Canine Cosmonauts

1   **LAIKA (RUSSIAN FOR "BARKER")** The first living creature to go into space was a mongrel stray plucked from obscurity on the streets of Moscow and rocketed to international fame aboard *Sputnik 2*, the space satellite launched from the Baikonur Cosmodrome in Kazakhstan on November 3, 1957. There was never any intention of bringing her back safely down to earth. Laika died in a state of panic and agony when the capsule overheated just a few hours after *Sputnik 2* was launched.

2 & 3   **BARS ("PANTHER") AND LISICHKA ("LITTLE FOX")** Killed on July 28, 1960, on board the Soviet *Vostok* spacecraft when their rocket booster exploded during launch.

4 & 5   **BELKA ("SQUIRREL") AND STRELKA ("LITTLE ARROW")** Launched into space on board *Sputnik 5* on August 19, 1960, accompanied by forty mice, two rats, and a number of plants. All were safely recovered after spending a day in orbit. President John F. Kennedy demanded to know why the world's first pair of space dogs were called Belka and Strelka and not Rover and Fido. Soviet scientists took note: After their hounds returned to earth, they bred puppies from Strelka and gave one to Kennedy. Ignoring warnings that the Russians may have hidden microphones inside the dog, the president ordered her life spared.

6 & 7   PCHELKA ("LITTLE BEE") AND MUSHKA ("LITTLE FLY") Launched on board *Sputnik 6* on December 1, 1960. The launch went well and the dogs spent a day in orbit, but there were problems with reentry and the rocket and its passengers were incinerated.

8   CHERNUSHKA ("BLACKIE") Launched on March 9, 1961, on board the spaceship Vostok, accompanied by a "dummy cosmonaut," mice, and a guinea pig. The flight was a success and Chernushka was recovered successfully.

9 & 10   VERTEROK ("BREEZE") AND UGOLYOK ("LITTLE PIECE OF COAL") Launched on February 22, 1966, on board *Kosmos 10*, returning safely on March 16 after a twenty-two-day flight, an all-time canine space record.

Ten Items Yet to Appear on eBay

I ADOLF HITLER'S TOILET SEAT In 1968, the lavatorial requisite allegedly belonging to the Führer was put up for auction in Los Angeles. The seller, a former U.S. fighter pilot named Guy Harris, claimed he rescued it from Hitler's bunker in 1945 because it was the only item he could find; everything else had been scavenged by Russian troops.

2 JEFFREY DAHMER'S REFRIGERATOR In 1996, the fridge in which Dahmer, "the Milwaukee Cannibal" serial killer, stored his victims' skulls was to be auctioned to settle claims made by the families of some of his victims. The sale was called off after a civic group, fearing bad publicity for their fair city, pledged to pay $407,225 for the famed cannibal's household appliance.

3 TOTO In 1996, the stuffed carcass of Toto, the dog who starred with Judy Garland in the 1939 film *The Wizard of Oz*, fetched $8,000 at auction.

4 LEE HARVEY OSWALD'S TOE TAG In 1992, the bloodstained toe tag from Oswald's corpse was sold at auction in New York for $6,600. The item was removed from Oswald by the ambulance driver as he drove him to the Dallas morgue.

5. BONNIE AND CLYDE'S HAIR In May 1934, the legendary bank robbers were ambushed in their car by a posse of patrolmen and perforated by seventy-seven bullets, which sprayed their brains all over the upholstery. The vehicle and its contents were quickly

trashed by local people hunting for trophies, including
locks of Bonnie Parker's hair. One man was apprehended
by a coroner as he attempted to saw off one of Clyde
Barrow's ears.

6   ANATOMICAL ARTIFACTS The surgeon John
Hunter, the unrivaled expert of eighteenth-century
anatomy, was a tireless collector of embalmed fetuses,
corpses, and human and animal skeletons. Over a period
of thirty years, Hunter amassed about 65,000 items. His
uncomplaining wife Anne is said to have registered a
protest only once when he brought home a stuffed giraffe
that was too tall to fit inside his house. Hunter shortened
it by hacking off the legs below the knees and placed it
in his hall. He bequeathed his collection to the Company
of Surgeons at Lincoln's Inn, London, but in May 1941
the building took a direct hit from a German bomber.
Only some 3,600 specimens were spared.

7   BLADDER STONES OF THE FAMOUS The finest
collection of bladder stones ever assembled by one man
was the pride and joy of Sir Henry Thompson, urologist
to the crowned heads of Europe. When Sir Henry died,
he bequeathed all one thousand of his bladder stones,
including a couple removed from Leopold I, king of the
Belgians, and France's Napoleon III, to the Royal College
of Surgeons in London.

8   EVA PERÓN'S SHROUD In 2004 the silk shroud
covering the embalmed remains of Eva Perón, wife of

the Argentine dictator Juan Perón, sold at auction for
$160,000.

9   THE LAST DYING BREATH OF THOMAS
     EDISON Henry Ford captured it in a bottle in 1931.

10   THE WORLD'S MOST EXPENSIVE TURD The
     most collectible piece of human ordure in history is a
     nine-inch stool known as the Lloyds Bank Turd. The
     unique Viking stool, so called because it was found in an
     archaeological dig under a Lloyds bank in the UK, is
     insured for $400,000. It is so highly valued because of its
     near-perfect condition, a rarity among thousand-year-old
     pieces of feces.

Ten Surprising Firsts

1   Buzz Aldrin was the first man to defecate on the moon.

2   Before he became the first to lose his head, Louis XVI was the first French king to use a knife and fork and to brush his teeth.

3   George Bush was the first U.S. president to be seen throwing up on live TV.

4   Joseph Stalin was the first dictator to have a theme park dedicated to him—Stalin World, ninety miles southwest of Vilnius in Lithuania.

5   Fatty Arbuckle was the first alleged rapist to have a chain of fast-food restaurants named after him.

6   Henry Laurens, a South Carolina statesman, was the first person to be formally cremated in the U.S., in 1792.

7   James Madison was the first president to wear long pants instead of knee breeches.

8   Frenchman Louis Sebastian Lenormand was the first man to use a parachute, in 1783. He tested it by dropping live domestic animals from the top of the tower of the Montpelier Observatory.

9   The first Frisbees were invented by children on the Oregon Trail, who flung discs of buffalo dung in a Frisbee-like manner during play.

10 The first World Testicle Cooking Championship was held in Serbia in 2004.

You Shouldn't Have:
Ten Great Gifts

1   During Christmas in 1888, Vincent van Gogh called at a Paris brothel with a present for a girl called Rachel and told her, "Keep it and treasure it." It was his ear.

2   The Dominican dictator Rafael Trujillo signaled the imminent death of an inner-circle adviser by awarding him the Christopher Columbus medal. It became a tradition after the first recipient of the Columbus medal died from tetanus because Trujillo inadvertently stuck him with the pin.

3   King Edward VII owned a golf bag made from an elephant's penis, a gift from an admirer, an Indian maharajah; it was a sly reference to Dirty Bertie's love of golf, hunting, and sex, but not necessarily in that order.

4   In 1995, Lord Erskine of Rerrick bequeathed his testicles to the Bank of Scotland (which had declared him bankrupt), because it had "no balls."

5   Pills made from the toxic metal antimony were highly esteemed in medieval times as bowel regulators. The pills irritated the intestinal tract, causing loose motions, and would pass through the body unharmed, so they could be handed down from father to son and from mother to daughter as precious family heirlooms.

6   Moulay Ismael, the sultan of Morocco, gave samples of his bowel movements to ladies of the court as a mark of special favor.

7   Pope Pius IX gave Queen Isabel of Spain, on the occasion of her birthday, the embalmed corpse of Saint Felix.

8   Warriors of the cannibalistic Brazilian Cubeo tribe gave their wives the penis and scrotum of a defeated victim. The wife was expected to eat them to make herself fertile.

9   The 1897 Sears, Roebuck & Co. mail-order catalog offered a selection of hypodermic syringe kits for shooting up heroin.

10   During a drug raid on a house party in Kansas in 1994, police officers found a mummified female head in a box marked "Eight-Piece Party Cook Kit." The head was wrapped in a white lab smock and had blond hair and eyebrows, but no brain. The owner, fifty-one-year-old Donald Donohue, said it was a gift from a medical student.

Ten Litigious People

1993   Vicki Daily of Jackson, Wyoming, runs over and kills a man while driving her pickup truck, then files a lawsuit against the dead man's widow. Lawyers acting for Ms. Daily say she expects compensation for the "grave and crippling psychological injuries" she suffered while watching the fifty-six-year-old victim die.

1993   A New York appeals court rejects housewife Edna Hobbs's lawsuit against a company that sold a sound-activated switching device, The Clapper. The complainant says that in order to turn her appliances on, she clapped until her hands bled. The judge found that Mrs. Hobbs had merely failed to adjust the sensitivity controls.

1994   Bernadette French, a thirty-six-year-old manic depressive, successfully sues the Wilmington Hospital in Delaware for $1.1 million. A judge rules that hospital staff had been very negligent in allowing her to gouge her own eyes out.

1994   Robert Jones, from Berkshire, England, files an insurance claim for the loss of his parrot. The recently deceased Polly, killed by Jones's dog, had been kept in the family freezer for posterity, but during a power cut had thawed and decomposed.

1994   A jilted Spaniard breaks into his ex-girlfriend's car in Barcelona and blows his own brains out with a gun. Vehicle owner Maria Valdez sues his family for ruining the interior of her car.

225

1995   Joel Ford from Jackson, Mississippi, files a $45 million
        lawsuit against the Oxford University Press, publishers of
        the principal edition of the Bible. Ford complains that
        the book is "based on hearsay" and "oppresses blacks and
        gays." He drops his action a few weeks later, however,
        claiming to have received death threats.

1996   A fifty-four-year-old truck driver files a $10 million
        lawsuit in Gallatin, Tennessee, after receiving a less-
        than-perfect penile implant. He claims he suffered
        blisters, bruising, infection, and embarrassment. An
        attorney explained: "He could be just walking down the
        street, and it would erect on its own."

1996   Popular Israeli Channel 2 weatherman Danny Rup is
        sued for $1,000 by a woman from Haifa. She was seeking
        damages after he predicted sunshine for a day that
        turned out wet and windy. Thanks to Rup's erroneous
        forecast, she left home lightly dressed and as a result
        caught the flu, which caused her to miss four days of
        work and spend $38 on medication.

1997   The journal *Biological Therapies in Psychiatry* reports
        that a thirty-five-year-old woman is claiming damages
        after her regular antidepressant was switched to
        bupropion. As a side effect of the new drug, the journal
        reports, she experienced spontaneously and without
        physical stimulation a three-hour orgasm while shopping.

1999   Donald Drusky from Pennsylvania receives the final
        rebuff in his thirty-year battle against his former

employees for "ruining his life" by firing him in 1968.
Drusky sued "God the sovereign ruler of the universe"
for "taking no corrective action" and demanded that the
Almighty compensate him with professional guitar-
playing skills and the resurrection of his late mother. A
federal judge in New York rejects the lawsuit.

T_{welve} Occupational Hazards

1. King John of Bohemia (1296–1346) became completely blind at the age of forty-four. When a team of palace surgeons failed to restore his eyesight, he had all of them drowned in the Danube.

2. In 1895, a dispute over trading rights resulted in an attack by more than a thousand angry tribesmen, led by King Koko, on the British-owned Niger Company in Akassa. The native chiefs later sent a letter to Britain, addressed to the Prince of Wales, expressing their deep regrets for having taken the law into their own hands, and especially for having eaten his employees.

3. The Ottoman sultan Mahomet IV (1648–87) appointed a historian called Abdi to write a running biography of his reign. One evening, the sultan asked Abdi if he had written about his reign that day. Abdi replied in the negative: Nothing particularly noteworthy had happened. Mahomet calmly picked up a hunting spear and impaled the scribe with it. "Now," he told Abdi, "thou has something to write about."

4. In 1994, the U.S. author Gavin Whitsett was mugged and badly beaten in Evansville, Indiana. He is chiefly known for writing a surprise best-seller, *Guerrilla Kindness: A Manual of Good Works, Kind Acts and Thoughtful Deeds*, which urges his fellow Americans to indulge in random and spontaneous acts of kindness.

5. In May 1994, a French clown, Yves Abouchar, choked to death after receiving a custard pie in his face from a colleague.

6   In the court of Imperial China, human wet nurses were trained to suckle the royal Pekingese puppies.

7   The ancient Egyptian pharaohs employed human fly-traps who were smeared with asses' milk and made to stand in a corner of the room.

8   The diamond company De Beers once employed security guards to undertake fingertip searches through the feces of their fellow employees to ensure that they weren't taking their work home with them.

9   The ancient Egyptians were martyrs to their bowels: Believing that all diseases were diet-related, they binged on laxatives such as castor oil, figs, and dates and purged themselves for three days at a time. The court official who supplied the enema to the pharaoh was given the title Shepherd to the Royal Anus.

10   The world's most difficult stand-up comic gig was performed by the eunuch dwarfs in the court of the Ottoman sultans. The dwarfs were required to keep the royal womenfolk amused while they gave birth.

11   In 1983, Mike Stewart, president of the Auto Convoy Company in Dallas, Texas, was standing on the back of a flatbed truck as it passed under a low bridge. He died instantly. At the time, he was fliming a TV item about the dangers of low bridges.

12   The body mass attained by Japanese sumo wrestlers—
      average weight around 320 pounds—renders many of
      them incapable of wiping their own backsides, a task that
      novice wrestlers are expected to perform for them. Six
      out of every ten novices run away from their workplace
      in the first year of apprenticeship.

T*e*n Election Fixes

1868: Thaddeus Stevens, a popular Republican congressional candidate from Pennsylvania, dies at age seventy-six. His party nominates him for the House of Representatives anyway as a belated tribute to "our most able and distinguished champion of justice." The corpse is elected with a large majority over its Democrat rival eight weeks later.

1928: The incumbent president of Liberia, Charles King, enjoys a landslide electoral victory, beating his rival, Thomas Faulkner, by more than 600,000 votes. The size of the victory is a surprise, as Liberia has only about 15,000 registered voters.

1955: South Vietnam is asked to choose between its former emperor, Bo Dai, and Ngo Dinh Diem, who is backed by the U.S., which calls him the best man to keep South Vietnam from falling under the control of Communism. France gives contrary advice, pointing out that Diem is "not only incapable but mad." When the voters arrive at the polling station, they are handed two ballot papers, red for Diem and green for Bo Dai; in Vietnamese tradition, red signifies good luck, green indicates bad fortune. Diem's supporters are also on hand to advise voters to put the red papers in the ballot box and to throw the green ones into the wastebasket; the few who do not take their advice are savagely beaten. Six Buddhist monks, demonstrating against Diem's corrupt rule, commit suicide in public by pouring gasoline over their heads and setting fire to themselves. Unmoved, Diem offers to supply all of his country's Buddhist monks with free gas.

1961: Haiti's president, "Papa Doc" Duvalier, takes his countrymen to the polls, where they find printed at the top of each ballot the words "Doctor François Duvalier, President." When the votes are counted, it is announced that Papa Doc has been unanimously reelected because his name appears on every ballot. A few years later, he uses a similar tactic to prolong his stay in office ad infinitum: When Haitian voters are asked, "Do you want your president elected for life?" the answer was a convenient and overwhelming "Yes"; the ballot did not include a "No" box.

1975: Philadelphian Frank O'Donnell is elected to serve on the city council despite his death from a heart attack a week before election day. A spokesman explains, "It seemed appropriate to remove his name from the ballot, but there just wasn't enough time."

1981: Saddam Hussein's war with Iran is going badly, and with morale low, he calls a meeting of his cabinet ministers and offers his resignation. Most take the hint and vote that he stay on. His health minister alone takes him up on the offer and votes for Saddam to step down. Saddam takes him into the next room, shoots him in the head, and sends the man's butchered remains home to his wife in a shopping bag.

1982: Texas Democrat John Wilson is elected to the Senate with 66 percent of the vote. Senator Wilson has been dead for two months, but his name could not be removed from the ballot sheet for "technical reasons."

1990: Frank Ogden III enjoys a surprise landslide local election victory in Oklahoma over Josh Evans. The loser, Evans, is disconsolate. He was convinced that his campaign slogan of being an "able lawyer and a living person" would give him the edge over Ogden, who had died three months before polling day.

1991: Texas state legislator Larry Evans is discovered dead in his Austin apartment. His demise causes some confusion when it emerges that although he has been dead for a week, according to House records, he voted on at least one measure that very day.

1996: The former mayor of the cult-dominated town of Rajneeshpuram, Oregon, confesses to organizing several deterrents to keep the noncult townspeople away from the ballot box during local elections. His methods include making them ill by tampering with the food at a local restaurant and coating courthouse doorknobs with a chemical irritant as election day approaches.

T*en* Short Leaders

1   King Pepin "the Short"—3' 6"

2   Pope Gregory VII—4' 1"

3   King Charles III of Naples—4' 5"

4   Attila the Hun—4' 6"

5   Queen Anne—4' 9"

6   Queen Victoria—4' 10"

7   King Emmanuel III of Italy—4' 11"

8   Alexander the Great—5'

9   Napoleon Bonaparte—5' 4"

10 Joseph Stalin—5' 4"

T*em* Heroic PR Campaigns

1   In 1994, the world's media descended on Gloucester, England, following the discovery of bodies in a "garden of death" belonging to Britain's then-biggest serial killers, Frederick and Rosemary West. Gloucester city fathers, upset by the negative publicity generated by the murders, decide to launch an advertising campaign to improve Gloucester's image. The Touchpaper agency emerges with the winning slogan, "Gloucester—easy to get to, hard to leave."

2   The slogan used by brewers Coors, "Turn It Loose," was translated into Spanish as "Suffer from Diarrhea."

3   The Ramses brand of condom is named after the great pharaoh Ramses II, a man who fathered more than 160 children. In the late nineteenth century, British condoms were illustrated with a portrait of Queen Victoria: She was a mother of nine.

4   Chicken magnate Frank Perdue's ad campaign was based on the slogan, "It takes a tough man to make a tender chicken." The Spanish translation came out as, "It takes a sexually stimulated man to make a chicken affectionate."

5   When the president of Haiti, "Papa Doc" Duvalier, discovered that tourism in his country was down by 70 percent, he found himself torn between his country's need for revenue and his natural and deep mistrust of foreigners. "Papa Doc" hit upon a compromise. He launched a publicity drive to tempt the visitors back,

then had the corpse of a dissident flown into the capital Port-au-Prince, where it was left to rot in public. It was strategically placed by an exit from the airport next to a sign that read "Welcome to Haiti."

6   Israel's notoriously reckless drivers kill about five hundred people per year. In 1994, a Tel Aviv advertising agency erected posters around the city chastising drivers with the message: "Research proves: Drivers who get rowdy on the road have small penises."

7   In 1994, Holland's National Liver and Intestine Foundation, which supports research on digestive problems, launched a publicity campaign encouraging people to fart fifteen times a day to ease intestinal discomfort.

8   When Gerber first started selling its baby-food products in Africa, it used the same packaging that had been so successful at home, featuring a baby on the label. The company was perplexed when it failed to get anywhere near projected sales figures, until someone pointed out that it is common practice in Africa to put pictures of the contents on food package labels.

9   Coca-Cola launched its product in China for the first time in the 1920s, unaware that its famous brand name translated literally as "Bite the wax tadpole." It was hurriedly changed to something that translated roughly as "happiness in the mouth." When Pepsi Cola was launched in China in the 1970s, the company's marketers

opted to play it safe with their award-winning slogan "Come alive with Pepsi." Predictably, however, it did not translate quite as intended, so the product was introduced to a quarter of the world's population with the line, "Pepsi brings your ancestors back from the grave."

10   A men's-underwear advertisement on billboards in Tel Aviv featured a photo of the late Israeli prime minister Golda Meir with the slogan, "Eventually we remember those who had balls."

Fat Cats and Top Dogs:
The World's Ten
Wealthiest Pets

1   GUNTHER IV, GERMAN SHEPHERD DOG
$328 million: German countess Karlotta Libenstein
left $109 million to her dog Gunther III when she
died in 1992, but clever trustees invested well and
tripled the fortune for Gunther III's pup.

2   KALU, CHIMPANZEE $96 million: Owner Patricia
O'Neill made a monkey of her husband, Australian
swimmer Frank, by changing her will while he was
away at the 2000 Sydney Olympics.

3   TOBY RIMES, POODLE $82 million: This
descendant of the original Toby, who inherited $27
million from the New York eccentric Ella Wendel in
1931, benefited from investments made by trustees.

4   GIGOO, HEN $18 million: The nest egg was left by
publisher Miles Blackwell after his wife Briony
predeceased him by a few weeks in 1999.

5, 6 & 7   FRANKIE, CHIHUAHUA; AND ANI AND PEPE
LE PEW, CATS $5.5 million each: The three
pampered pets live in an $18 million San Diego
mansion while their caretaker, Lerissa Patrick, lives in
a small adjoining apartment.

8 & 9   HELLCAT AND BROWNIE, CATS $3.6 million
each: Offspring of the original fat cats Hellcat and
Brownie, who inherited $750,000 from San Diego
owner Dr. William Grier.

10   MOOSE, JACK RUSSELL TERRIER $3.3 million:
Better known as Eddie on *Frasier*, he earned $11,000
per episode.

T*en* Francophobes

1 "You must consider every man your enemy who speaks ill
of your king: and you must hate a Frenchman as you
hate the devil."
—Lord Horatio Nelson

2 **Guillotine,** n. A machine which makes a Frenchman
shrug his shoulders with good reason.
—Ambrose Bierce, Devil's Dictionary

3 "The French; utter cowards who force their own children
to drink wine, they gibber like baboons even when you
try to speak to them in their own wimpy language . . .
racial characteristics; sawed-off cissies who eat snails and
slugs and cheese that smells like people's feet."
—P. J. O'Rourke, National Lampoon 1976

4 "I remember being much amused last year, when
landing at Calais, at the answer made by an old traveler
to a novice who was making his first voyage. 'What a
dreadful smell,' said the uninitiated stranger, enveloping
his nose in his pocket handkerchief. 'It is the smell of
the continent, sir,' replied the man of experience. And so
it was."
—Mrs. Frances Trollope

5 "France is a dog-hole, and it no more merits the tread
of a man's foot."
—William Shakespeare, All's Well That Ends Well

6 "France is a country where the money falls apart in your
hands and you can't tear the toilet paper."
—Billy Wilder

7   "There's always something fishy about the French!
      Whether Prince or Politician
      We've a sinister suspicion
      That behind their savoir-faire
      They share
      A common contempt
      For every mother's son of us."
    —Noël Coward, from Conversation Piece

8   "Having to go to war without France is sort of like
    having to go deer hunting without an accordion."
    —Ross Perot

9   "There is no hell. There is only France."
    —Frank Zappa

10   "Cheese-eating surrender monkeys."
    —Bart Simpson

Now Wash Your Hands:
Ten Rules of Etiquette

1   According to British royal etiquette, men suffering from ringworm are not obliged to remove their hats in the presence of the monarch.

2   It is traditional for Russian cosmonauts to urinate on a tire of the bus that takes them to the launchpad, a custom initiated by Yuri Gagarin.

3   In Nepal, Narikot wives are obliged to wash their husbands' feet, then drink the dirty water as a token of their devotion.

4   The typical greeting of Masai tribesmen is to spit at each other.

5   In sixteenth-century Europe, it was customary for men to greet female guests by fondling their breasts, provided they were related.

6   The sixteenth-century Danish astronomer Tycho Brahe died after attending a banquet hosted by a baron in Prague. Brahe drank heavily, but etiquette prevented him from leaving the table to relieve himself before the host left. His bladder burst and he died of a urinary infection eleven days later.

7   Nineteenth-century sailors in the British Royal Navy were forbidden to eat with forks because the utensils were considered unmanly.

8   Fijian cannibals usually ate with their hands, but as a token of respect for the dead, they used a ritual wooden fork when consuming people.

9   In accordance with the ancient Indian laws of Manu, any
     citizen who broke wind in front of the monarch was
     likely to have his anus amputated.

10   The African dictator Idi Amin dispensed advice on
     protocol to his fellow world leaders, from President
     Richard Nixon to Mao Zedong. He once reminded Israeli
     prime minister Golda Meir to pack her underpants.

Ten Awesome
Compensation Claims

1   $1 billion: the amount claimed in 1998 by Cairo lawyer
    Mustafa Raslan in Damanhur, Egypt, against President
    Clinton. Raslan alleged that Clinton's widely reported
    sexual peccadilloes made it impossible for him to raise
    his own children with good moral standards.

2   $9 million: paid by the New York Transit Authority in
    1990 to a restaurant worker who fell in front of a train
    while drunk and lost an arm.

3   $6.6 million: claimed in 1997 by a Californian, who sued
    the owners of a house he had rented after he hurt
    himself diving into their swimming pool. They had
    failed to warn him that it also had a shallow end.

4   $3.6 million: damages claimed by Ursula Beckley of
    Long Island against a local supermarket in 1989 after the
    three-egg omelets she was making suddenly yielded an
    unexpected bonus in the form of a healthy, six-inch-long
    black snake. Her lawyers said that she had been so deeply
    traumatized that it was unlikely she would ever be able
    to look at an egg again.

5   $2.52 million: awarded to a convenience-store worker in
    West Virginia in 1995 after she suffered emotional
    distress, having hurt her back while opening a pickle jar.

6   $2 million: awarded to a convicted bank robber on parole
    in Oakland, California, in 1987, when the wad of money
    he had recently stolen from the Savings and Loan
    Company exploded in his pocket, releasing tear gas and
    dye and causing burns that required hospital treatment.

7    $1 million: claimed against Robert Nelson, president of a
     U.S. company that offered a cryogenics service,
     preserving in capsules of liquid nitrogen the bodies of
     people prepared to pay large sums in the hope that one
     day science will find a cure for death. In 1981, Nelson
     and an employee, Joseph Klockgether, were successfully
     sued for damages by relatives of their clients after
     admitting that they had allowed the frozen loved ones to
     thaw out.

8    $1 million: the amount claimed against Disneyland in
     1997 by a woman who complained that her
     grandchildren were traumatized by seeing Mickey Mouse
     climb out of his costume.

9    $100,000: received in damages in 1998 by Englishman
     Charles Cornell in the High Court, London. The
     plaintiff's insurance businesses failed following his car
     accident. In the crash, Carnell received head injuries that
     his doctors testified left him with a gentler, more amiable
     personality, which was unsuited for the insurance
     business.

10   $50,000: received in a 1995 out-of-court settlement by a
     New Hampshire teenager from the manufacturers of a
     basketball net. The complainant lost his two front teeth
     when they became entangled in the net while he was
     performing a slam dunk.

$E\mathcal{leven}$ Unexpected Origins

1560: Jean Nicot, a French ambassador in Portugal, gives his name to the remarkable new wonder drug nicotine, an antiseptic and universal cure-all that will put an end to ulcers, bites, headaches, colds, and rheumatism. A distinguished English doctor hails Monsieur Nicot's discovery as "one of the best and surest remedies in the world" for apoplexy and giddiness.

1585: Sir Walter Raleigh returns home with tobacco and potatoes from the New World. It is generally agreed that potatoes are a potential health hazard leading to scrofula, consumption, flatulence, and unnatural carnal lust.

1859: Vaseline is invented in Brooklyn, New York, by a young English-born chemist, Robert Chesebrough. Ideal for removing stains from furniture, polishing wood surfaces, restoring leather, and preventing rust, it is also useful for dressing cuts and bruises. Chesebrough recommends eating a spoonful every day for good health: He ate a spoonful every morning and died at the age of ninety-six.

1876: Ketchup is marketed in the U.S. as a patent medicine to cure dyspepsia, liver and kidney complaints, and constipation.

1880: Opium is recommended as a cure for cholera, dysentery, toothache, flatulence, menopause, and mental illness and is the basis for several baby-soothing remedies.

1886: John Pemberton, an Atlanta pharmacist, stumbles upon the recipe which would become Coca-Cola. At the time, he is working on series of failed patent medicines and hair restorers, including Triplex Liver Pills, Indian Queen Hair Dye, and Globe of Flower Cough Syrup.

1894: Dr. Harvey Kellogg creates his first breakfast-cereal product as an antidote to masturbation.

1898: Bayer, the company famous for manufacturing aspirin, launches Heroin, a new patent cough medicine. The new wonder drug, made from synthesized morphine, is also used to "cure" morphine addiction, to send babies with colic to sleep, and as a general painkiller; it is the subject of an intense advertising campaign at the turn of the century. Within twenty years, New York has fewer hacking coughs, but an estimated 300,000 heroin addicts.

1910: Salversan, the first effective treatment for syphilis, is invented by the admirably persistent Paul Ehrlich. Popularly known as "Treatment 606," it is Ehrlich's six-hundred-and-sixth attempt to find a cure.

1931: A Colorado physician, Dr. Earle Cleveland Haas, obtains a patent for his invention, Dr. Haas' Catamenial Device. After early indifference to his project, he changes the name to Tampax, created from the words "tampon" and "vaginal pack."

1932: Adolf Hitler sketches a design for a new car on his napkin at a Munich restaurant table. He calls it the "Strength through Joy" car: It later becomes known as the Volkswagen Beetle.

T*en* Zealous Officials

1. When the city of Kirtipur in Ceylon fell to the king of Ghorka in 1770, the victor ordered an accurate census of the population. His officials obliged by amputating, then counting, the noses of everyone there.

2. In 1994, the regulatory authority for funeral parlors in Massachusetts suspended the license of undertaker Robert Miller for two years. It was acting on complaints that he had dug up the remains of two cremated bodies because relatives of the deceased failed to pay their funeral bills promptly.

3. In 1994, in Riga, Latvia, five local bus inspectors beat a thirty-three-year-old man to death for failing to produce a valid bus ticket.

4. In 1994, Los Angeles city officials ordered a strip-club owner to remove the stage upon which nude dancers performed. The authorities ruled that the stage was not wheelchair-accessible for disabled nude dancers, although they admitted that no such dancers had yet come forward.

5. In preparation for the first death-row hanging in fifty years, that of convicted murderer William Bailey in 1996, officials at the Delaware Correctional Center fixed nonskid safety strips to each of the twenty-three steps leading to the outdoor gallows.

6. In 1994, the Pennsylvania State Weights and Measures Office served notice of a violation on topless dancer Crystal Storm. They had ascertained that Miss Storm's

bust measurement was only 50 inches, not her advertised measurement of "127," which Miss Storm later claimed was in centimeters.

7   In 1992, the South Carolina Social Services Department sent a letter to a recently deceased man, informing him: "Your food stamps will be stopped effective March 1992 because we received notice that you passed away. May God bless you. You may reapply if there is a change in your circumstances."

8   In the nineteenth century, Indian tax collectors persuaded defaulters to pay up by forcing them to drink buffalo milk laced with salt until they were half-dead with diarrhea.

9   In 1988, Cynthia Hess, who worked under the stage name "Chesty Love" in Indiana, claimed a $2,088 tax deduction against depreciation on surgical breast implants, weighing about ten pounds each, which boosted her bust size to 56FF. Tax officials allowed her claim: Ms. Hess's breasts, they agreed, were so large that she couldn't possibly derive any personal benefit from them and therefore were for business use only.

10   A man who died in his car in November 2005 was given a parking ticket as he sat slumped in his vehicle outside a busy shopping center in Melbourne, Australia. The traffic warden stuck the infringement notice on the seventy-one-year-old man's car at Croydon Market. The mayor of the local council admitted: "It's a sad situation. But it is simply a case of the parking officer not noticing."

Chapter Nine

End Notes

T*en* Deaths Without Dignity

456 B.C.: Aeschylus, the father of Greek tragedy, dies when an eagle drops a tortoise on his head.

1649: Sr. Arthur Aston (c. 1590–1649), the Royalist commander during the English Civil War, is beaten to death with his own wooden leg by Cromwell's men during the siege of Drogheda.

1687: Jean-Baptiste Lully, the French composer, accidentally stabs himself in the foot with his baton and dies of gangrene.

1737: Queen Caroline, wife of King George II, shows remarkable composure during a badly bungled attempt to cure her neglected strangulated hernia, but as she lies in bed surrounded by courtiers, her bowels burst, showering a torrent of excrement over the bed and the floor. Upon her death soon afterward, the poet Alexander Pope is moved to write:

Here lies wrapt in forty thousand towels
The only proof that Caroline had bowels.

1845: At President Andrew Jackson's funeral, his pet parrot, Poll, has to be ejected from the proceedings when it swears repeatedly.

1927: Isadora Duncan, the American dancer, having just taken delivery of her brand-new Bugatti racing car, steps into it for the first time, waves gaily to her friends, and speeds away. As she does so, her long red scarf becomes entangled in the spokes of her left rear wheel, snapping her neck and killing her instantly.

1975: Claude François, "the French Elvis Presley" and co-writer of one of the most successful songs of all time, "My Way," dies attempting to change a lightbulb while standing in a water-filled bath, age thirty-nine.

1995: An Italian stripper, Gina Lalapola, is found suffocated inside a cake she was supposed to leap out of at a bachelor party in Cosenza. Her body had lain inside the sealed wooden cake for more than an hour before her death was discovered.

1998: The family of the late Russell U. Shell files a wrongful-death lawsuit against The Other Side nightclub in Fitchburg, Massachusetts, after Shell chokes to death on a miniature plastic penis in his cocktail.

2005: Reverend Kyle Lake, thirty-three, reaches for a microphone while standing in a pool used for a Sunday-morning baptism in Waco, Texas, and is electrocuted. Pastor Ben Dudley tells the press: "At first there was definitely confusion just because everyone was trying to figure out what was going on, but then everyone just immediately started praying."

Twelve Famous Body Parts

1. SANTA ANNA'S LEG The hero of the Alamo had a leg torn off in a skirmish with the French, but recovered it. When he eventually became president of Mexico, he gave the limb a full state funeral. At public events he rode on horseback, waving his new cork leg over his head as a symbol of his sacrifices for his country. In 1847, facing the United States at the Battle of Cerro Gordo in Mexico, Santa Anna was enjoying a quiet roast-chicken lunch when his appetite was ruined by an uninvited regiment of Illinoisans, who stole the cork prosthetic. Santa Anna hobbled away to fight another day, but the iconic limb remained in American hands, despite many requests from the Mexican government that it be returned. In the 1850s, army veterans charged a nickel or a dime for curiosity-seekers to handle the leg in hotel bars. Santa Anna's trophy of war now resides in the Guard's Museum at Camp Lincoln in Springfield.

2. ALBERT EINSTEIN'S EYES Although officially he was cremated and his ashes were scattered in the Delaware River, Einstein's death led to an unseemly scramble for his body parts. Removed by his ophthalmologist Dr. Henry Abrams during the autopsy in 1955, the peepers were stored in a safe-deposit box in a New Jersey bank.

3. NAPOLEON BONAPARTE'S PENIS Removed at autopsy by a team of French and Belgian doctors, the member has been put up for auction twice, first in 1972 at Christie's in London, when it was observed to be approximately one inch long and was listed as "a small

dried-up object." It failed to measure up to the reserve price and was withdrawn, but was bought five years later by an American urologist for $3,800.

4   ADOLF HITLER'S TEETH Discovered by Soviet soldiers in a shallow grave outside his Berlin bunker in 1945 and used to positively identify his charred remains, they have remained locked away in an archive in Moscow ever since.

5   ELVIS PRESLEY'S WART The ultimate in Elvis memorabilia, removed from his right wrist in 1958; it is currently owned by Joni Mabe of Athens, Georgia.

6   JOSEPH HAYDN'S HEAD The great composer was buried headless when two of his best friends bribed the gravedigger to let them have it as a keepsake. For nearly sixty years it was stored in a cupboard in the Museum of the Vienna Academy of Music, but it was reunited with the rest of his remains in 1954.

7   SIR WALTER RALEIGH'S HEAD After Raleigh's execution in 1618, his head became a family heirloom. His widow, Elizabeth, kept it for twenty-nine years before willing it to their son Carew, who looked after it until 1666, when it went with him to his grave.

8   KING CHARLES XII OF SWEDEN'S SKULL Now on permanent public display in Stockholm, the skull reveals the large bullet hole that made the exhibition possible in 1718.

9   BOB MARLEY'S HAIR In May 2003 a ten-inch lock
      of hair from the reggae legend was sold at auction for
      $5,000. The seller was a fan who had asked the singer for
      a souvenir dreadlock backstage in 1980.

10   KING CHARLES I'S FOURTH CERVICAL
      VERTEBRA The novelist Sir Walter Scott broke the ice
      at parties by introducing dinner guests to his novelty salt
      shaker, made from a relic stolen by a surgeon during an
      autopsy on the royal corpse after Charles's long-lost coffin
      was rediscovered at Windsor Castle in 1813. Scott kept it
      on his dining table for thirty years until Queen Victoria
      heard about it. She was quite unamused and ordered that
      it be returned to St. George's chapel.

11   CHARLES BABBAGE'S BRAIN The nineteenth-
      century mathematician known as the "Father of
      Computing" died in 1871, mostly forgotten and unloved,
      his groundbreaking work on computers gathering dust in
      the Museum of King's College, Cambridge. In 1908, after
      being preserved for thirty-seven years in alcohol,
      Babbage's brain was dissected by Sir Victor Horsley of
      the Royal Society. Horsley was obliged to remind his
      colleagues that Charles Babbage had once been a "very
      profound thinker."

12   CANCEROUS TISSUE FROM THE JAW OF U.S.
      PRESIDENT GROVER CLEVELAND This resides in
      the Mutter Museum of Philadelphia, which specializes in
      bizarre medical curiosities, in the company of the B. C.

Hirot Pelvis Collection, the Sappey Collection of
mercury-filled lymphaticus, the Chevalier Johnson
collection of foreign bodies removed from lungs, and
the joined liver of Chang and Eng Bunker, the original
Siamese twins.

T𝑒𝘯 Great Grave Robberies

1.   Benito Mussolini's corpse is stolen from its supposedly secret, unmarked grave in a municipal cemetery by Fascists intent on a publicity stunt and nostalgic for his regime. A message left in the grave read: "Finally, O Duce, you are with us. We will cover you with roses, but the smell of your virtue will overpower those roses." Four months later, what remained of Il Duce was found in a small trunk just outside Milan, and two Franciscan monks were charged with hiding his body. In the intervening months the corpse had been kept on the move, variously hidden in a villa, a monastery, and a convent. Il Duce was buried a second time in an undisclosed location, only to be dug up yet again eleven years later and returned to his widow, Rachele, who buried him yet again in Predappio in 1957.

2.   The tomb of King Richard I at Westminster Abbey once had a hole in it, through which visitors could actually touch his skull. In 1776, a schoolboy stole the king's jawbone; it was kept as a family heirloom until it was finally returned to the abbey in 1906.

3.   When King Henry VIII was interred in the royal vault at Windsor, a workman removed one of his finger bones and used it to make a knife handle.

4.   Oliver Cromwell's skull has changed hands many times since the Lord Protector lost exclusive use of it in 1658. After the restoration of the monarchy, Cromwell's corpse was exhumed from Westminster Abbey and hanged at Tyburn. It was then taken down from the scaffold and

decapitated. The body was thrown into a pit beneath the gallows, the head set on a spike above Westminster Hall. The head remained there for forty-three years until it was dislodged in a violent storm and was found lying on the ground by a sentry. He took it home and kept it hidden in his chimney, and on his death he left it to his daughter. In 1710 the head reappeared, this time in a freak show. By 1775 it had been sold to an actor named Russell, who in turn sold it in 1787 to James Fox, an antique dealer. Fox sold it for £230 (about $440) to three men who put it on display in Old Bond Street, London, and charged half a crown per viewing. By 1865, it had passed into the possession of a Mr. Williamson of Beckenham. His family donated it to Sydney Sussex College in the 1960s. At one time there were even two "authentic" Cromwell skulls on sale in London simultaneously. The owner of the second, smaller skull explained that his version was obviously that of Cromwell when he was a boy.

5   While Galileo's corpse was being moved to its final resting place in a mausoleum in Santa Croce, Florence, in 1737, the antiquary Anton Francesco Gori helped himself to the middle finger of the great astronomer's right hand. The digit is now displayed in the Museum of the History of Science in Florence in a glass egg on top of a plinth. The inscription below states that the famous digit *"nunquam visos mortalibus orbes / Monstravit"*— "pointed out bodies never seen by mortals before."

6   In 1790, the remains of the poet John Milton were raided by souvenir hunters at St. Giles Cripplegate. A woman gravedigger, Elizabeth Grant, was later found to be charging visitors sixpence apiece for viewings of Milton's teeth and part of his leg.

7   In 1876, an American gang was apprehended while attempting to steal the remains of Abraham Lincoln. They were going to hold the body for ransom in return for the release of a convicted forger, Ben Boyd. To deter any more raids, Lincoln's coffin was embedded in steel and concrete.

8   In 1895, General Horatio Herbert Kitchener was sent to avenge the death of the British war hero General "Chinese" Gordon, who was killed at Khartoum by the troops of the Sudanese leader, known as the Mahdi. As the Mahdi was already dead, however, Kitchener had to content himself with gratuitous desecration by blowing up the Mahdi's tomb at Omdurman and throwing his bones into the Nile. Kitchener also planned to keep the Mahdi's skull as an inkwell; Queen Victoria heard about Kitchener's trophy and ordered him to return it immediately.

9   The hands of the Argentinean president General Juan Perón were amputated in 1987 and subject to a $9 million ransom demand. Fortunately Perón had no further use for them, as he had already been dead for thirteen years.

10   In March 1978, the body of Charlie Chaplin was stolen
      from its grave in Vevey, Switzerland, and held for a
      600,000-franc ransom by a Pole, Roman Wardas, and a
      Bulgarian, Gantcho Ganev. The body snatchers were
      finally arrested, and Chaplin's remains were retrieved
      from a cornfield a few miles away. They said they needed
      the money to start a garage business.

T*en* Failed Suicides

63 B.C.: King Mithradates VI, who rules in Asia Minor, deliberately takes small doses of poison in the hope that he will build up enough resistance to survive a possible assassination by poisoning. He finally gets an opportunity to see if his regimen has worked when, in an attempt to take his own life rather than fall into the hands of invading Romans, he tries to poison himself. His body is so full of toxins, however, that the poison has no effect at all, and the king has to order a slave to finish him off with his sword.

1744: Robert, Lord Clive "of India" (1725–74) twice fails to shoot himself. After the second attempt, he declares, "It appears I am destined for something. I will live."

1826: While in the care of his guardian uncle, Ludwig, the depressed Karl von Beethoven pulls out a gun and fires two shots at his own head. One shot misses completely, the other grazes his temple.

1848: Edgar Allan Poe attempts suicide by taking an ounce of opium, which is rejected by his stomach.

1854: Robert Schumann leaves a house full of visitors in his nightgown and throws himself into the Rhine River, but is rescued by some boatmen. His wife Clara places him in an insane asylum.

1877: Two weeks after his wedding, Piotr Ilyich Tchaikovsky stands in the Neva River up to his armpits, hoping to catch a fatal bout of pneumonia. He is rescued by his brother, who takes him home suffering from a slight chill.

1878:   Joseph Conrad, plagued by financial problems, shoots himself in the chest but misses all vital organs.

1898:   Paul Gauguin, suffering from syphilis and living in poverty, attempts suicide after completing his painting "Where Do We Come From? What Are We? Where Are We Going?" He takes arsenic, but swallows too much and immediately vomits it back up.

1932:   While living at the Algonquin Hotel, Dorothy Parker, distraught over a breakup with her young boyfriend and suffering from writer's block, makes her fourth suicide bid by swallowing barbiturates, which only results in vomiting and stomach cramps. Three previous failed attempts involved slashing her wrists, overdosing on the sedative Veronal, and drinking a bottle of shoe polish.

1982:   Salvador Dalí, distraught at the death of his wife, Gala, attempts suicide by deliberately dehydrating himself. He fails, although it does help speed up his subsequent cremation when he eventually dies from heart failure.

Ten Instant Dismissals

1. The fifteenth-century German emperor Wenceslas had his cook roasted on a spit when the cook's normally exemplary meals fell below standard. On another occasion, Wenceslas was out hunting when he came across a passing monk and shot him dead: The emperor explained that monks had better things to do than wander about in woods.

2. Henry VIII invented a new method of execution for Richard Rosse, cook to the Bishop of Rochester, who had poisoned the soup at a formal banquet and killed seventeen people. The king had him boiled to death in one of his own stockpots.

3. King Gustavus I of Sweden hacked his royal goldsmith to death because the man had taken a day off without permission.

4. King George II suffered terribly from hemorrhoids and an anal fistula but was very vain and notoriously touchy about his ailments, which were supposed to be a secret. When one of his lords of the bedchamber tactlessly inquired after the king's health, George fired him on the spot.

5. In 1994, a twenty-six-year-old stripper, Lisa Evans, claimed unfair dismissal against the owners of a nightclub in Edmonton, Alberta, where she had worked in a nude peep-show booth. Management said customers had complained because the 270-pound stripper was difficult to fantasize about.

6   In 1996, a Madras train announcer, Rajiv Kamir, was fired for making farting noises over the PA system to the tune of the opening of Beethoven's Fifth Symphony. A railroad spokesman noted, "It was a disgusting deviation from the timetable."

7   In 1996, the county coroner in Tacoma, Washington, was removed from his post following complaints that he had encouraged his employees to make sexually explicit jokes about corpses and that he allowed them to circulate photographs of the private parts of deceased prominent local people.

8   In 1994, the U.S. neurosurgeon Dr. Raymond Sattle was removed from his post after he left a patient alone on the operating table with his brain exposed for half an hour while he went out for his lunch break in the middle of aneurysm surgery. The North Carolina Board of Medical Examiners heard that Dr. Sattle also frequently forgot the names of his surgical equipment during operations, allowed an untrained nurse to drill holes in a patient's head, and had fluids pumped into his own veins while he was operating to help him stay on his feet.

9   Forty-one-year-old Milton Ross was fired from his desk job in St. Joseph, Montana, in 1994 after a video camera recorded him urinating into the office coffeepot. The video trap was set after his colleagues noted that their morning coffee seemed "off."

10   In 1993, Susan Franano, the general manager of the Kansas City Symphony Orchestra, fired oboist Ken Lawrence after he made a "facetious response" to a complaint about him. During a rehearsal for *The Nutcracker*, Lawrence had farted loudly, "creating an overpowering smell."

T*em* Ex-Hypochondriacs

1   ARISTIDES (AD 117–180) Greek orator and bedridden disciple of the healing god Asclepius. Died of natural causes at age sixty-three.

2   DR. SAMUEL JOHNSON (1709–84) Often begged his wife to lock him in his room and shackle his legs, convinced he was going mad. Died of natural causes at age seventy-five.

3   JAMES BOSWELL (1740–95) The friend and famous biographer of Samuel Johnson wrote a series of seventy essays in the *London Magazine* offering advice to fellow hypochondriacs and suggesting ways they might "distract" themselves from their morbid preoccupation. A heavy drinker and regular VD sufferer, he died of a fever at age fifty-five.

4   QUEEN VICTORIA (1819–1901) Summoned her court physician up to six times a day. He was surprised to receive a telegram from the queen while he was away on his honeymoon, informing him, "The bowels are acting fully." Died in her sleep at age eighty-two.

5   FLORENCE NIGHTINGALE (1820–1910) After her return home at the end of the Crimean War, she took to her bed, where she more or less remained for the rest of her life. Died of natural causes at age ninety.

6   IMMANUEL KANT (1724–1804) The German philosopher spent a lifetime meticulously recording details of his "Diatetik"—a strict diet intended to ensure

long life—and his bodily fluids. He died after prolonged illness at age eighty.

7   ROBERT BURNS (1759–96) Suffered ill health all his adult life. Died of bacterial endocarditis secondary to chronic rheumatic heart disease at age thirty-seven.

8   CHARLES DARWIN (1809–82) Took to his bed for months at a time with an awe-inspiring list of ailments, including gastrointestinal pain, nausea, vomiting, sleeplessness, headaches, and giddiness. Died of heart disease at age seventy-three.

9   ALFRED, LORD TENNYSON (1809–92) Queen Victoria's favorite poet, he succeeded William Wordsworth as poet laureate in 1850. Plagued by imagined illness, Tennyson didn't write a line of poetry for ten years but sought a cure through hydropathy, a method of "treatment" in which the patient is doused with cold water. Died of natural causes at age eighty-three.

10   LEO TOLSTOY (1828–1910) Sexually active into his eighties, he died of a chill shortly after leaving his wife at the age of eighty-three.

Where There's a Will:
Ten Last Testaments

1   The most generous last will and testament of all was left
by Ecuadorian Indian endo-cannibals—cannibals who
eat and are eaten by members of their own family. Their
wills gave express details of which body parts were to be
eaten by which lucky relatives. As soon as the will was
read, the funeral became a banquet as the corpse was
roasted, cut into pieces, and consumed by grieving
relatives. The head was generally kept until it was ripe
with maggots; then the brains were eaten with spices.

2   William Shakespeare left his wife Anne Hathaway his
"second-best bed."

3   Ernest Digweed, a teacher from Portsmouth, England,
died in 1976, leaving his entire assets of $43,000 to Jesus
Christ in the event of his second coming. If Christ has
not appeared to claim his bequest by 2056, the whole
amount will revert to the state.

4   One of the strangest acts of philanthropy ever was the
last will and testament of the London miser John
Camden Neild, who left his fortune of $9.5 million
(about $50 million in today's value) to Queen Victoria,
who was already one of the richest women in the
country. She kept every penny while continuing to harass
the government for more money. Her relatively poverty-
stricken uncle, King Leopold of Belgium, wrote to
congratulate her on her windfall, noting "Such things
only still happen in England."

5   In 1862, Henry Budd leaves $386,000 in trust for his two
sons on the condition that neither grows a moustache.

6   In 1975, the Mrs. Martin van Butchell, the wife of a London dentist, repaid her husband for years of marital misery with a spiteful will that decreed that her fortune pass to a distant relative "the moment I am dead and buried." The resourceful dentist, however, kept the money by simply leaving her body well above ground. Van Butchell persuaded a skilled embalmer to fit her out with a new pair of glass eyes and filled her veins with oil of turpentine and camphorated spirit of wine. She was then dressed, propped up in the drawing room, and put on public display from 9 a.m. to 1 p.m. from Monday to Saturday. The rush to see the corpse was so great that van Butchell was forced to restrict viewings to private appointments only. He remarried and, not surprisingly, his second wife, Elizabeth, took an instant dislike to the ex-Mrs. van Butchell and ordered her out of the house. Reluctantly, the dentist gave the mummy to a museum. By about a century later, it had disintegrated into a "repulsive-looking object." It was only in 1941——166 years after her death——that she was finally laid to rest when the museum took a direct hit from a German incendiary bomb.

7   When the mistress of the nineteenth-century French novelist Eugène Sue died, she willed him her skin with instructions that he should bind a book with it. He did.

8   The philosopher Jeremy Bentham thought that burying the dead was a wasteful business. He suggested that everyone should be embalmed and preserved as his or her own commemorative bust or statue: He called them

"auto-icons." The possibilities, Bentham posited, were endless: Portraits of ancestors could be replaced by actual heads, "many generations being deposited on a few shelves or in a modest-sized cupboard." When Bentham died, he put his money where his mouth was by leaving his body to medical science, to be dissected, embalmed, dressed in his own clothes, and placed in a glass case. His head was replaced by a wax version, however, when it took an unfortunately grim expression during the embalming process. Bentham's physician, Dr. Southwood Smith, kept the body until his own death in 1850, when it was presented to University College, London.

9   When D. H. Lawrence died, in accordance with his last wishes his wife Frieda had his ashes tipped into a concrete mixer and incorporated into her new mantelpiece.

10 In 1910, a Swede, Olav Olavson, in exchange for a lump sum, willed all rights to his body to the Karolinska Institute for medical research after his death. The following year, Olavson had an unexpected and massive windfall and tried to buy himself back. The Institute refused to sell and went to court to verify its claim. The court upheld the claim; and, as Olav had since had two teeth pulled without seeking its permission, the Institute was also awarded damages.

T*en* Royal Deaths

1. AGATHOCLES, FOURTH-CENTURY KING OF SICILY Believed to have been paralyzed by a poisoned toothpick, is laid out on his funeral pyre alive.

2. KING JAMES II OF SCOTLAND While he inspected one of his own cannons, it exploded and a piece of shrapnel sliced the top of his head off.

3. EMPEROR MENELIK II OF ETHIOPIA In 1913, convinced that he could cure illness by eating pages from the Bible, he had a stroke and died while attempting to eat the entire Book of Kings.

4. CHARLES VIII OF FRANCE Fatally cracked his head on a low wooden beam while entering a tennis court.

5. FREDERICK, PRINCE OF WALES, HEIR TO GEORGE II Caught a slight chill and died suddenly a few weeks later at age forty-four. His death was said to have been aggravated by an old cricketing injury.

6. KING ALEXANDER I OF GREECE Died of blood poisoning after being bitten by his pet monkey.

7. CZAR PETER III While under house arrest following a palace coup, he was strangled. However, according to the official announcement, he died from "an acute attack of colic during one of his frequent bouts of hemorrhoids."

8. EMPEROR MAXIMILIAN I OF MEXICO Shot by a local firing squad of Mexican revolutionaries. Maximilian begged his executioners to shoot him cleanly so that he could die with dignity, but they were poor

shots and their bullets blew off most of his face. Parts of his body were allegedly auctioned to souvenir hunters.

9   EMPRESS ELIZABETH OF AUSTRIA Stabbed to death in Geneva by an Italian anarchist, Luigi Lenchini. The killer later confessed that he had nothing at all against the empress and had actually set out to kill King Umberto I of Italy but hadn't been able to afford the extra fifty lire he needed to travel to Rome.

10 KING ALEXANDER AND QUEEN DRAGA OF SERBIA Overthrown by a Serbian army coup. Finding the king and queen hiding in a palace-bedroom wardrobe, soldiers sprayed them with bullets, hacked them to pieces with swords, bashed in their skulls with rifle butts, and then tossed their corpses out the window into the gardens below. A few of the queen's relatives who got in the way were slaughtered for good measure.

It's Your Funeral: Ten Reasons Why You May Wish You Had Died in Ignorance

1   According to the medical profession, the five most
    reliable methods of diagnosing death are:

    (a) Pouring freezing water in your ear
         (should provoke an eye-movement in the living)
    (b) Poking something into your eye
         ("testing the corneal reflex")
    (c) Poking something down your throat
         ("testing the gag reflex")
    (d) Grinding knuckles into your sternum
         ("testing the pain reflex")
    (e) Squeezing your testicles (see d).

    If none of these techniques elicits a response, you are
    probably deceased.

2   A corpse left above ground in warm weather will be
    reduced to a skeleton in about nine days. The rate of
    decay varies, because fat people decompose more quickly
    than thin people: The extra flab retains body heat, which
    speeds up the bacterial process that breaks down body
    tissue.

3   **As your corpse dissolves**, your skin color may change
    from green, to purple, to black. Rigor mortis starts in
    your feet and travels upward.

4   Embalmers use Superglue to prevent your mouth from
    falling open. A coating of softened wax is also applied to
    both the upper and lower lip to prevent cracking and
    flaking.

5   To avoid any possibility of insects entering your body via your nose, your nostrils are deeply packed with cotton wool that is saturated with a liquid insecticide.

6   The putrefaction process releases gases that can make the body swell to two or three times its normal size in twelve to eighteen hours, and the pressure of accumulating methane can cause internal organs to be forced out of the lower orifices. Embalmers always check your abdominal and thoracic regions for any signs of distension or bloating caused by gaseous buildup, then relieve pressure by opening an anal vent.

7   Fingernails and hair do not continue to grow after death. This myth arose from the illusion created by skin retracting around the hair and nails, which makes them stand up and stick out more prominently.

8   Until the 1950s, coffins were hardly ever made to measure. If your body didn't fit your coffin, the undertaker would normally break your ankles and bend your feet back.

9   The cremated remains of most adults will weigh between 2.5 and 8 pounds. The difference is due to bone size, not live weight.

10   Because of the high water content of the average human adult, cremation is tricky even with modern furnaces. Modern crematoriums are equipped with electrically operated crushing machines designed to pulverize

unburnt bones. In some undeveloped countries, however, bodies are first wrapped in layers of animal fat to aid combustion. In India, many families can't afford enough fuel to do the job properly, and half-burned bodies are often thrown into a river.

T_e_n Postmortem Adventures

1   Mark Gruenwald, the Marvel Comics editor who helped
     create Captain America, requested that his ashes be
     mixed with ink and printed into a comic book after his
     death. His remains were accordingly printed into a
     special edition poster of Squadron Supreme in 1996.

2   In 1999, the cremated remains of *Star Trek* creator Gene
     Roddenberry and LSD advocate Dr. Timothy Leary were
     launched into space on a Spanish research satellite.

3   Ed Headrick, the man who invented the Frisbee,
     requested that his ashes be cast into a series of limited-
     edition discs.

4   Elizabeth, the wife of the poet and painter Dante Gabriel
     Rossetti, died in 1862, accidentally overdosing on the
     laudanum she was taking for neuralgia. Rossetti was
     grief-stricken and, as a token of his love, had a pile of his
     unpublished manuscripts wrapped in her long, golden
     hair and buried with her in her coffin. Seven years later,
     however, he had a change of heart and decided he
     wanted them back. Up came Elizabeth, and the poems
     were dusted off and published to great critical acclaim.

5   The guillotine held a morbid fascination for the French
     medical profession, who marveled at the speed of
     execution and speculated whether or not the brain would
     continue to function after decapitation. Some thought
     that the razor-sharp blade struck the victim so cleanly
     that they lost their heads before they knew anything
     about it, a theory fueled by dozens of stories about

victims who continued to protest after they had lost their heads. Eyewitnesses recorded that when the head of Jean Paul Marat's assassin, Charlotte Corday, was held up and slapped by the executioner, it showed unmistakable signs of anger. French doctors were allowed to carry out various experiments on severed heads, including pinching the cheeks, sticking things up the nostrils, holding lighted candles near the eyeballs, and even shouting the victim's name very loudly in the ear of the severed head. In 1880, experimenters pumped the blood of a live dog into the head of the murderer Menesclou. It was recorded that the head responded with a look of "shocked amazement."

6   A nineteenth-century German missionary, Reverend Schwartz, was revived by the sound of his favorite hymn being played at his funeral. Mourners were said to be "surprised" when the prematurely buried priest joined in the singing from within his coffin.

7   When the author Thomas Hardy died, it was his wish that his final resting place should be his birthplace, Stinsford. The authorities, however, decreed that he was far too important for such a humble interment. A compromise was reached: It was decided that most of Hardy's remains should be sent to Westminster Abbey, but that his heart could be buried at Stinsford. On the morning of the ceremony, his sister inadvertently left the open casket with the heart on the kitchen table and the contents were consumed by the family cat.

8   Lenin has been dead since 1924, but Russia's most
        popular embalmee has still managed to get through
        several dozen new suits. Under his tailored blue acrylic
        three-piece, the father of Communism also wears a
        rubber wetsuit, into which is poured the solution that
        keeps him from falling apart. Twice a week the parts that
        show—his hands and face—are painted with fresh
        embalming fluid, and every eighteen months the whole
        body is lifted out and given a good soaking. Every four
        years, a sample of Lenin's skin is scraped off and
        microscopically examined for signs of deterioration. An
        estimated 60 percent of his body is now made of wax,
        including his ears: The original pickling was botched and
        bits of him have "gone off" since. He also sports a
        growth of fungus around his neck and the back of his
        head that definitely wasn't there when he led the
        Bolsheviks to power in 1917. When Communism was still
        popular, Lenin had to be refrigerated with equipment
        from a German fish-freezing plant to stop his body parts
        from melting from the body heat of visiting tourists.

9   Because of a fault in the embalming process, the body of
        Chairman Mao Zedong is apparently shrinking at a
        steady rate of about 5 percent a year. The official line
        given by the mausoleum director is that this is merely an
        optical illusion caused by the curious lighting effects in
        the hall that contains his corpse.

10   William the Conqueror, or William the Bastard as he was
        known out of earshot, survived a a lifetime of warring
        and bloodletting to die at the ripe old age of sixty, when

his horse stumbled on hot cinders, thrusting the corpulent king against the iron pommel, mashing his left testicle and causing fatal internal injuries. There was worse to come. His body was carried to Caen in France, but a fire broke out and the coffin-bearers had to rush off to fight the blaze. Eventually the procession continued, but William's rotting corpse had been forced into a stone coffin that was far too small; this, combined with a stifling hot day, caused the corpse to explode and the cathedral had to be evacuated. In 1562, looters stole everything from William's tomb, including most of his body. Eighty years later, a new monument was built containing all that remained of William—a thighbone.

Ten Lavatorial Deaths

1   **ROMAN EMPEROR ELAGABALUS (218–222 AD)** Hacked to death by the Praetorian Guard as he sat on the toilet. His body was thrown down a Roman sewer.

2   **KING EDMUND II "IRONSIDE"** Murdered in 1016 by a Dane, armed with a long sword, who was hiding in a cesspit beneath the wooden royal commode.

3   **KING HENRY III OF FRANCE** Stabbed to death as he sat on the toilet by a Dominican friar, Jacques Clément, egged on by the pope, who had excommunicated the French king, calling him "an assassin, a heretic, and an infidel."

4   **RUSSIAN EMPRESS CATHERINE "THE GREAT"** Died of heart failure while straining to overcome constipation.

5   **KING GEORGE II** According to his German valet, one evening a roar emanated from the palace toilet that he judged to be "louder than the usual royal wind," and he found the king dead on the floor. George had fallen off the toilet and smashed his head on a cabinet.

6   **LUPE VELEZ** In 1934, this thirty-six-year-old Hollywood screen actress, known as the "Mexican Spitfire," attempted suicide by overdosing on sleeping pills but miscalculated the required dosage and merely got violently sick. As she made a dash for the bathroom, she slipped on the tiled floor and was flung headfirst into her toilet bowl. Her maid found her the next day with her head jammed into the bowl, drowned.

7   KING HAAKON VII OF NORWAY In 1957, he slipped on soap in his marble bathroom and smashed his head on some taps, fatally fracturing his skull.

8   JUDY GARLAND Found dead by her fifth husband, Mickey Devinko, on June 21, 1969, sitting on her toilet. Official cause of death: accidental barbiturate poisoning.

9   ELVIS AARON PRESLEY The King died of heart failure on August 17, 1977, while straining to overcome constipation on his Graceland throne.

10 MICHAEL ANDERSON GODWIN Having spent several years awaiting South Carolina's electric chair for murder, Godwin had his sentence reduced to life in March 1989. Shortly afterward, attempting to fix his TV set, he bit into a wire while sitting on a metal toilet in his cell and was electrocuted.

No Nearer My God to Thee:
Quotes from *Twenty*
Dead Atheists

1   DAVID HUME, SCOTTISH PHILOSOPHER
    (1711–76) "When I hear a man is religious, I conclude
    that he is a rascal."

2   NAPOLEON BONAPARTE, FRENCH EMPEROR
    (1769–1821) "Religion is excellent stuff for keeping
    common people quiet."

3   THOMAS JEFFERSON, AMERICAN PRESIDENT
    (1743–1826) "Religions are all alike–founded upon
    fables and mythologies . . . the day will come when the
    mystical generation of Jesus, by the Supreme Being as
    His father, in the womb of a virgin, will be classed with
    the fable of the generation of Minerva in the brain of
    Jupiter."

4   PERCY BYSSHE SHELLEY, ENGLISH POET
    (1792–1822) "If God has spoken, why is the world not
    convinced?"

5   KARL MARX, GERMAN POLITICAL
    PHILOSOPHER (1818–83) "Religion is the sigh of the
    oppressed creature, the heart of a heartless world, and
    the soul of soulless conditions. It is the opium of the
    people."

6   OSCAR WILDE, IRISH AUTHOR (1854–1900)
    "When I think of all the harm the Bible has done, I
    despair of ever writing anything to equal it."

7   MARK TWAIN, AMERICAN AUTHOR
    (1835–1910) "It ain't the parts of the Bible that I can't

understand that bother me, it is the parts that I do
understand."

8 THOMAS HARDY, ENGLISH AUTHOR (1840–1928)
"After two thousand years of mass, we've got as far as
poison gas." (poem, Christmas 1924)

9 FRIEDRICH NIETZSCHE, GERMAN
PHILOSOPHER (1844–1900) "God is dead."

10 THOMAS EDISON, AMERICAN INVENTOR
(1847–1931) "Religion is all bunk."

11 SIGMUND FREUD, PIONEER PSYCHOANALYST
(1856–1939) "In the long run, nothing can withstand
reason and experience, and the contradiction religion
offers to both is palpable."

12 GEORGE BERNARD SHAW, IRISH PLAYWRIGHT
(1856–1950) "The fact that a believer is happier than a
skeptic is no more to the point than the fact that a
drunken man is happier than a sober one."

13 BERTRAND RUSSELL, BRITISH PHILOSOPHER
(1872–1970) "Religion is based ... mainly on fear ...
fear of the mysterious, fear of defeat, fear of death. Fear
is the parent of cruelty, and therefore it is no wonder if
cruelty and religion have gone hand in hand."

14 ALBERT EINSTEIN, SCIENTIST (1879–1955) "I do
not believe in a personal God and I have never denied
this but have expressed it clearly. If something is in me
which can be called religious then it is the unbounded

admiration for the structure of the world so far as our science can reveal it."

15   ROBERT BURNS, SCOTTISH POET (1759–96) "Of all nonsense, religious nonsense is the most nonsensical."

16   VICTOR HUGO, FRENCH AUTHOR AND DRAMATIST (1802–85) "There is in every village a torch—the schoolmaster, and an extinguisher—the parson."

17   ERNEST HEMINGWAY, AUTHOR (1899–1961) "All thinking men are atheists."

18   W. C. FIELDS, ACTOR (1880–1946) "Prayers never bring anything. They may bring solace to the sap, the bigot, the ignorant, the aboriginal, and the lazy, but to the enlightened it is the same as asking Santa Claus to bring you something for Xmas."

19   GENE RODDENBERRY, CREATOR OF *STAR TREK* (1921–91) "Religion is nothing more than a substitute for a malfunctioning brain."

20   SAMUEL BECKETT, IRISH-BORN WRITER (1906–89) "The bastard! He doesn't exist!" (*Endgame*)

Dying Optimists:
Ten Last Words

1   "I think I could eat one of Bellamy's veal pies."
    —William Pitt the Younger, British prime minister, 1801

2   "Sergeant, the Spanish bullet isn't made that will kill me."
    —William "Bucky" O'Neill, American war hero, 1898

3   "It's nothing."
    —Franz Ferdinand, Austrian archduke, 1914

4   "I'm getting better."
    —D. H. Lawrence, British author, 1930

5   "Get my swan costume ready."
    —Anna Pavlova, Russian ballerina, 1931

6   "I think I'm going to make it."
    —Richard A. Loeb, American playboy
    and convicted murderer, 1936

7   "I've never felt better."
    —Douglas Fairbanks Sr., American actor, 1939

8   "Die? I should say not, dear fellow. No Barrymore would allow such a conventional thing to happen to him."
    —John Barrymore, American actor, 1942

9   "Go away. I'm all right."
    —H. G. Wells, British author, 1946

10 "Do you know where I can get any shit?"
    —Lenny Bruce, American comedian, 1966

Twelve Suggestions
for Further Reading

1   *The Romance of Leprosy* by E. Mackerchar, 1949

2   *Why Bring That Up? A Guide to and from Seasickness* by J. F. Montague, 1936

3   *Penetrating Wagner's Ring* by John L. Digaetani, 1978

4   *Jews at a Glance* by Mac Davis, 1956

5   *Constipation and Our Civilization* by J. C. Thomson, 1943

6   *A Pictorial Book of Tongue Coating* —Anon., 1981

7   *A Government Committee of Enquiry on the Light Metal Artificial Leg* by Captain Henry Hulme & Chisholm Baird, 1923

8   *Daddy Was an Undertaker* by McDill, McGown, and Gassman, 1952

9   *A Short Account of the Origin, Progress and Present State of the New Rupture Society* —Anon., 1816

10   *Amputation Stumps: Their Care and After-treatment* by Sir Godfrey Martin Huggins, 1918

11   *A Study of Masturbation and Its Reputed Sequelae* by J. F. W. Meagher, 1924

12   *Sex After Death* by B. J. Ferrell and D. E. Frey, 1983

KARL SHAW is the author of *Gross: A Compendium of the Unspeakable, Unpalatable, Unjust and Appalling* and *Royal Babylon: The Alarming History of European Royalty.* He lives in Staffordshire, England.

THE ROLLICKING EXPOSÉ THAT LEAVES NO THRONE UNSPURNED

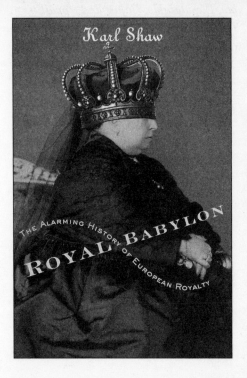

Karl Shaw

THE ALARMING HISTORY OF EUROPEAN ROYALTY

ROYAL BABYLON

European royalty brims with history lessons you weren't taught in school. Like the one about the empress who kept her dirty underwear under lock and key. Here at last is the eye-opening dish on hundreds of years of royally bizarre behavior. Karl Shaw's *Royal Babylon* will have you gasping and guffawing—and suddenly feeling more optimistic about democracy.